A Thyme to Celebrate

FRESH, CLASSIC RECIPES FOR ALL OF LIFE'S CELEBRATIONS

A Cookbook by the Junior League of Tallahassee

A Thyme to Celebrate

FRESH, CLASSIC RECIPES FOR ALL OF LIFE'S CELEBRATIONS

Published by the Junior League of Tallahassee, Inc.
Copyright © 2009 by
The Junior League of Tallahassee, Inc.
404 East 6th Avenue
Tallahassee, Florida 32303
850-224-9161

Photography: © by Gjergj Ndoja, Volaj Photography, LLC

Food Styling: Gjergj and Hester Ndoja

Wine Pairings: Lee Satterfield

Nutritional Information: Barbra Crumpacker, RD, Archbold Memorial Hospital

Tallahassee Information: Tallahassee Area Convention & Visitors Bureau

Tallahassee Trivia: Gerald Ensley, *Tallahassee Democrat* columnist

This cookbook is a collection of our favorite recipes, which are not
necessarily original recipes.

Library of Congress Control Number: 2009924294
ISBN: 978-0-9620166-2-2

Edited, Designed, and Produced by

 Favorite Recipes® Press

An imprint of

FRP.INC

A wholly owned subsidiary of
Southwestern/Great American, Inc.
P.O. Box 305142
Nashville, Tennessee 37230
1-800-358-0560

Art Director and Book Design:
  Starletta Polster
Project Editor: Tanis Westbrook

Manufactured in the
United States of America
First Printing: 2009
10,000 copies

Proceeds from the sale of *A Thyme to Celebrate* are returned to the
community through the Junior League of Tallahassee's support of
community volunteer projects. The Junior League of Tallahassee is a
nonprofit organization of women committed to improving the lives of
children and families.

Foreword from Art Smith

Happy 50th Birthday to the Junior League of Tallahassee! Thanks to many tireless volunteers, the League has touched countless lives in the capital city area. The organization is to be commended on the many good deeds it bestows on others.

It is with a humble heart that I accept the invitation from the Junior League of Tallahassee (JLT) to write the foreword for its newest cookbook, *A Thyme to Celebrate*, which follows the successes of past JLT cookbook endeavors. Growing up in a small rural town in Florida, I was surrounded by great cooks, and many of my closest times with family and friends were centered around the table and wonderfully delicious food. It is there that I began my life's mission as a chef and an entrepreneur. It is also there that I realized the importance of food in our culture and how it truly brings people together. *A Thyme to Celebrate* reinforces my philosophy. Life is meant to be celebrated whether it is an intimate dinner for two, a large gathering to congratulate someone's accomplishments, or the special holidays and occasions that we share. Think of all the recipes that have been passed from generation to generation, all used for those special times of celebrating our own traditions.

I urge you all to take time to enjoy the simple pleasures of life by celebrating all that is important and good to you. Use this fabulous new cookbook, *A Thyme to Celebrate*, to bring your family and friends together and enjoy those times you will share gathering over good food.

Art Smith

Renowned Chef, Author, and Television Personality

Celebrating Our Supporters

A Thyme to Celebrate would not have been possible without our supporters.

Rowland Publishing

Capital City Bank

Leigh Ansley Catering

Realtors Political Action Committee

The Cottage Collection

Dr. and Mrs. Cory Couch

Gregg and Gina Colley-Holgate

Comedy Zone

Dr. Walter Colón and Marybeth Colón

Red Elephant Pizza and Grill Restaurant

Calynne Hill

Carter and Molly Kellogg

Chris and Amy Kise

Cindy Wise

Dr. Michael J. Caire

Ed and Melissa Lombard

Greenscapes Design & Company

In Tents Events

John W. Hartsfield, C.P.A., P.A.

Karl David and Michelle Lamar-Acuff

Mart P. Hill

Martha Olive Hall

Rick and Pam Edwards

Rowe Drilling Company

Susan McAlister

Barbra Crumpacker, Registered Dietitian, Archbold
    Memorial Hospital

Coton Colors

deVine Wine and Tasting Bar

Gjergj Ndoja, Volaj Photography, LLC

Mama and Baby LOVE

Tallahassee Area Convention & Visitors Bureau

Target Copy

John and Beth Kuhfuss

Dr. and Mrs. A. C. McCully

Lori Mattice

Margaret A. Johnson

Marilynn York Evert

Peggy Wells Hughes

Peoples First Community Bank

Junior League of Tallahassee

Our Mission

THE JUNIOR LEAGUE OF TALLAHASSEE is a nonprofit organization of women committed to improving the lives of children and families through the effective action and leadership of trained volunteers. Its purpose is exclusively educational and charitable.

Our Mark on the Community

ESTABLISHED IN 1960, the Junior League of Tallahassee (JLT) has served North Florida in numerous ways. With a diverse membership of more than 600 women, JLT has created new and innovative approaches to offering individual talents and valuable time toward improving the lives of children in our community. You will see evidence of the Junior League of Tallahassee's many projects throughout the years at Tallahassee Museum, Tallahassee Memorial Hospital, Refuge House, LeRoy Collins Public Library, the Mary Brogan Museum of Art & Science, and many more places around our community. For more information about the Junior League of Tallahassee, please visit www.jltallahassee.org.

Cookbook Committee

Chairs	Betsy Caire Couch and Gina Colley-Holgate
Celebrity Chef Coordinators	Nancy Click and Calynne Hill
Fund-raising/Sponsorships	Amanda Clements, 2008–2009 Cookbook Committee, and 2008–2009 Junior League of Tallahassee Board of Directors
Marketing Coordinator	Ivette Marques
Marketing Committee	Stephanie Brandt, Heather Harrington, and Elizabeth Moya
Partnership Coordinators	Sarah Zieman Martinez and Rian Meadows
Proofreader	Jennifer Blalock
Recipe Researcher	Lori Rowe
Recipe Chapter Coordinators	Alexis Antonacci Lambert Paige Benton Amy Cliburn Lily Etemadi Laureen McElroy Amanda Karioth Thompson
Recipe Tasting Coordinator	Jill Hoover
Recipe Tasting Committee	Amy Kirby, Lauren Patrick, and Amanda Porter
Secretary	Joanie Deibert Trotman
Special Effects Coordinator	Hester Cowles Ndoja
Special Events Coordinator	Stephanie Brandt
Sustainer Advisors	Calynne Hill and Lily Etemadi
Treasurer	Amy Cliburn

A Thyme to Celebrate

Break·fast &
Brunch

[brek·fuh st] & [bruhnch]

1. First meal of the day; usually
accompanied by orange juice, coffee,
and the morning news.

Quiche Lorraine

1 (1-crust) pie pastry
1 tablespoon butter, softened
12 slices bacon
4 eggs, beaten
1 1/2 cups heavy whipping cream
1/2 teaspoon salt
1/2 teaspoon pepper
1/8 teaspoon nutmeg
1 1/4 cups (5 ounces) shredded
  Swiss cheese

Preheat the oven to 425 degrees. Fit the pastry into a 9-inch pie plate, fluting the edge. Spread with the butter. Chill in the refrigerator. Cook the bacon in a skillet over high heat until brown and crisp. Remove to paper towels to drain and cool. Crumble the bacon into the pastry-lined pie plate.

Whisk the eggs, cream, salt, pepper and nutmeg in a bowl. Stir in the cheese. Pour over the bacon. Bake for 15 minutes. Reduce the oven temperature to 325 degrees. Bake for 45 to 55 minutes or until a wooden pick inserted in the center comes out clean. Remove from the oven and let stand for 10 minutes before serving.

LAURIE HARTSFIELD

Photograph for this recipe appears on page 8.

Quiche Florentine

1 (1-crust) pie pastry
1 tablespoon butter
6 ounces fresh baby spinach
3 eggs
1 (7-ounce) jar marinated
  artichoke hearts, drained
  and chopped
1 cup (4 ounces) shredded
  Swiss cheese
3/4 cup milk
1/4 teaspoon salt
1/8 teaspoon pepper

Preheat the oven to 350 degrees. Remove the pie pastry from the refrigerator and let stand for 15 minutes. Fit into a 9-inch pie plate, fluting the edge. Melt the butter in a medium skillet over medium-high heat. Add the spinach and sauté until wilted. Remove from the heat to cool. Chop the spinach.

Beat the eggs in a medium bowl. Add the artichoke hearts, cheese, milk, salt, pepper and sautéed spinach and mix well. Pour into the pastry-lined pie plate. Bake for 1 hour or until a wooden pick inserted in the center comes out clean. Remove from the oven and let stand for 10 minutes before serving.

NANCY CAIRE MILLER

Ham and Swiss Quiche

SERVES 8

1 teaspoon olive oil
1 (1-crust) pie pastry
5 eggs
2 cups (8 ounces) shredded baby
  Swiss cheese
1 1/2 cups finely chopped ham
1 1/4 cups milk
1 teaspoon dill weed
1/2 teaspoon salt
1/4 teaspoon pepper

Preheat the oven to 350 degrees. Brush a 9-inch pie plate with the olive oil. Fit the pastry into the prepared pie plate, fluting the edge. Place on a baking sheet. Combine the eggs, cheese, ham, milk, dill weed, salt and pepper in a large bowl and mix well. Pour into the pastry-lined pie plate. Bake for 45 minutes or until the center is set and the edge is golden brown.

KRISTIN M. LARGE

Spinach Squares

SERVES 6 TO 8

3 eggs
1 cup 2% milk
1 cup all-purpose flour
1 teaspoon baking powder
1 teaspoon salt
1 small onion, chopped
6 to 8 mushrooms, chopped
2 (10-ounce) packages frozen
  spinach, thawed and excess
  moisture removed
4 cups (16 ounces) extra-sharp
  Cheddar cheese, shredded

Preheat the oven to 350 degrees. Beat the eggs in a large bowl. Add the milk gradually, beating constantly. Add the flour, baking powder and salt and mix well. Add the onion and mushrooms and mix well. Stir in the spinach and then the cheese. Pour into a 9×13-inch baking pan sprayed with nonstick cooking spray. Bake for 35 minutes. Let cool slightly before cutting into squares.

KELLY BARBER

THYME SAVER

When you spray nonstick cooking spray into a pan, do it in the sink. Any overspray will be caught and washed clean the next time you do the dishes.

Feta Cheese and Leek Tart

1 1/3 cups all-purpose flour
1 bunch fresh chives, thinly
   sliced, or 3 scallions,
   thinly sliced
1/2 teaspoon paprika
1/4 cup (1/2 stick) butter
8 ounces feta cheese
3 to 4 tablespoons ice water
1 tablespoon olive oil
6 small leeks or 3 large leeks
   (white portions only), rinsed
   and coarsely chopped
1 garlic clove, minced
1/2 teaspoon salt
Freshly ground black pepper
   to taste
1 cup half-and-half
2 eggs
Pinch of cayenne pepper

Mix the flour, one-half of the chives and the paprika in a medium mixing bowl. Cut in the butter and 2 ounces of the cheese with a pastry blender until the mixture resembles coarse crumbs. Mix in enough of the ice water gently to hold the pastry together. The pastry can be prepared in a food processor.

Knead the pastry lightly on a lightly floured surface and shape into a ball. Roll into an 11-inch circle. Line a lightly greased 10-inch tart pan or a 9-inch pie plate with the pastry, trimming the edge. Chill for at least 1 hour. Preheat the oven to 375 degrees. Prick the pastry with a fork. Bake for 10 minutes.

Heat the olive oil in a skillet over medium heat. Add the leeks and garlic and reduce the heat. Cook, covered, until softened and golden brown. Stir in the salt and black pepper. Remove from the heat and set aside.

Whisk the half-and-half, eggs and cayenne pepper in a bowl until smooth. Brush the prebaked crust with a small amount of the egg mixture. Bake for 2 minutes. Sprinkle the leek mixture and the remaining chives in the tart shell. Crumble the remaining cheese evenly over the chives. Pour the remaining egg mixture over the top. Place on a baking sheet and bake for 25 to 30 minutes or until puffed and brown.

ORIGINALLY PUBLISHED IN *Thymes Remembered*

Western Breakfast Casserole

SERVES 4 TO 6

1 white baguette
1 pound hot bulk pork sausage
1/2 cup minced onion
1/2 cup chopped green
   bell pepper
5 eggs
2/3 cup milk
1/2 cup chopped tomato
1 cup (4 ounces) shredded sharp
   Cheddar cheese

Preheat the oven to 375 degrees. Cut the baguette into 1/4- to 1/2-inch slices. Lay the slices cut side down in a 21/2-quart baking dish until the bottom of the dish is evenly covered. Cook the sausage in a skillet over medium heat for 5 minutes or until brown, stirring until crumbly. Add the onion and bell pepper. Cook for 5 minutes or until the onion is cooked through. Spoon evenly over the bread.

Whisk the eggs, milk, tomato and cheese in a bowl briskly for 1 minute. Pour evenly over the sausage mixture. Bake for 35 to 45 minutes or until bubbly. Sprinkle an additional 1/2 cup cheese over the top if desired and bake for 2 to 3 minutes or until the cheese melts.

ALLISON KINNEY

Breakfast Pizza

SERVES 8

1 pound bulk pork sausage
1 pound maple bacon
10 eggs
1 large pizza crust
2 tablespoons olive oil
1 (8-ounce) jar salsa
4 cups (16 ounces) shredded
   Mexican cheese blend
2 cups (8 ounces) shredded sharp
   Cheddar cheese

Preheat the oven to 350 degrees. Brown the sausage in a large skillet over medium-high heat, stirring until crumbly. Drain and set aside. Fry the bacon in the skillet until brown and crisp. Remove the bacon to paper towels to drain. Drain the excess drippings from the skillet. Scramble the eggs in the skillet and set aside.

Brush the top of the pizza crust with the olive oil and place on a baking sheet. Bake for 7 to 10 minutes or until the top begins to crisp. Remove from the oven. Spread the salsa over the crust. Sprinkle generously with some of the Mexican cheese blend and Cheddar cheese. Crumble the sausage over the cheese layer. Crumble the bacon over the sausage and spread the scrambled eggs over the top. Sprinkle with the remaining Mexican cheese blend and Cheddar cheese. Bake for 20 to 30 minutes or until heated through.

Sausage Hash Brown Casserole

SERVES 12

1 pound mild bulk pork sausage

3 cups frozen or refrigerator shredded hash brown potatoes, thawed, drained and pressed

1/4 cup (1/2 stick) butter, melted

3 cups (12 ounces) mild Cheddar cheese, shredded

1/2 cup chopped onion

16 ounces small curd cottage cheese

6 jumbo eggs

Preheat the oven to 375 degrees. Brown the sausage evenly in a large deep skillet over medium-high heat, stirring until crumbly. Drain and set aside. Mix the potatoes and butter in a bowl. Line the bottom and sides of a lightly greased 9×13-inch baking dish with the potato mixture. Combine the sausage, Cheddar cheese, onion, cottage cheese and eggs in a bowl and mix well. Pour evenly over the potato mixture. Bake for 40 minutes or until a wooden pick inserted in the center comes out clean. Remove from the oven and let cool for 5 minutes before serving.

Hash Brown Casserole

SERVES 10

1/4 cup (1/2 stick) butter

1/2 cup chopped onion

1 (10-ounce) can cream of chicken soup

1 cup sour cream

1 cup (4 ounces) shredded Cheddar cheese

1 cup (4 ounces) shredded mozzarella cheese

1 (32-ounce) package frozen cubed or shredded hash brown potatoes

1 teaspoon salt

1/2 teaspoon pepper

1/4 cup (1 ounce) shredded Cheddar cheese

1/4 cup (1 ounce) shredded mozzarella cheese

Preheat the oven to 350 degrees. Melt the butter in a large saucepan over medium heat. Add the onion and sauté for 5 minutes. Stir in the soup, sour cream, 1 cup Cheddar cheese and 1 cup mozzarella cheese. Heat until the cheeses melt, stirring constantly. Remove from the heat. Add the hash brown potatoes, salt and pepper and mix well. Spoon into a 9×13-inch baking dish sprayed with nonstick cooking spray. Sprinkle with 1/4 cup Cheddar cheese and 1/4 cup mozzarella cheese. Bake, covered with foil, for 30 minutes. Remove the foil and bake for 30 minutes.

GLORIA MORGAN

Scrumptious Strata

1 (8-count) can refrigerator flaky
  dough sheet or 1 refrigerator
  crescent dough sheet
$1/4$ cup chopped onion
1 cup chopped red bell pepper
1 cup chopped yellow
  bell pepper
1 tablespoon butter
1 cup chopped ham
4 eggs
$1/2$ cup half-and-half
$1/2$ teaspoon salt
$1/2$ teaspoon pepper
2 cups (8 ounces) shredded
  Mexican cheese blend

Preheat the oven to 375 degrees. Unroll the dough sheet. Press over the bottom and halfway up the sides of a 9×13-inch baking dish. Sauté the onion and bell peppers in the butter in a skillet over medium heat for 5 minutes or until soft. Add the ham. Cook for 2 to 3 minutes or until heated through.

Beat the eggs lightly in a bowl. Add the half-and-half, salt, pepper and 1 cup of the cheese and mix well. Stir in the ham mixture. Pour into the prepared baking dish and sprinkle with the remaining 1 cup cheese. Bake for 45 minutes or until the center is set.

LIGHTEN UP

Small changes here and there in this classic strata will add up to big savings in both fat and calories in this healthier version: Use reduced-fat crescent rolls, or eliminate a little more by using refrigerator breadsticks as the base instead. Using evaporated skim milk and egg substitute and decreasing the amount of cheese skims fat while maintaining the scrumptious taste.

Barbecued Shrimp and Grits

1 1/2 cups (3 sticks) butter, chopped

1 cup vegetable oil

2 tablespoons chopped garlic

2 tablespoons paprika

1 1/2 teaspoons salt

2 tablespoons chopped fresh rosemary

1 teaspoon dried basil

1 teaspoon dried oregano

1 teaspoon cayenne pepper

2 teaspoons lemon juice (about 1 lemon)

2 pounds shrimp, peeled and deveined

Country Grits (below)

Melt the butter with the oil in a large deep skillet. Add the garlic, paprika, salt, rosemary, basil, oregano, cayenne pepper and lemon juice and mix well. Simmer for 30 minutes, stirring occasionally. Add the shrimp. Sauté until the shrimp turn pink. Remove from the heat and stir in the Country Grits. Make this the day before to let the flavors meld.

AGGIE BELL AND TRICIA WILLIS

Country Grits

3 1/2 cups water

2 cups heavy whipping cream

1 1/4 cups quick-cooking grits

1 tablespoon plus 1 1/2 teaspoons garlic powder

1 1/2 teaspoons onion powder

1 1/2 teaspoons salt

1 tablespoon Worcestershire sauce

1/2 teaspoon Tabasco sauce

1/2 cup canned cream-style corn

1/2 teaspoon pepper

Bring the water and cream to a boil in a large saucepan over medium-high heat. Add the grits, garlic powder, onion powder, salt, Worcestershire sauce, Tabasco sauce, corn and pepper and mix well. Simmer for 10 minutes or until thickened, stirring frequently.

AGGIE BELL

Blueberry Breakfast Casserole

1 loaf egg bread
16 ounces cream cheese,
  cut into cubes
1 cup fresh blueberries
12 eggs
2 cups milk
1/3 cup maple syrup
Blueberry Syrup (below)

Preheat the oven to 350 degrees. Cut the bread into cubes. Arrange one-half of the bread cubes in a 9×13-inch baking pan sprayed with nonstick cooking spray. Layer the cream cheese cubes and blueberries over the bread cubes. Cover with the remaining bread cubes. Beat the eggs, milk and maple syrup in a bowl. Pour evenly over the layers. Cover with foil and chill for 8 to 10 hours. Bake for 30 minutes. Uncover and bake for 30 minutes longer or until puffed and golden brown. Serve with Blueberry Syrup.

LEIGH ANSLEY CATERING

Blueberry Syrup

MAKES 3 CUPS

1 cup sugar
1 cup water
2 tablespoons cornstarch
1 cup fresh blueberries
1 tablespoon butter

Mix the sugar, water and cornstarch in a saucepan. Cook over medium-high heat for 5 minutes or until thickened, stirring occasionally. Add the blueberries. Simmer for 10 minutes. Add the butter. Cook until the butter melts, stirring constantly. Serve over Blueberry Breakfast Casserole, waffles or pancakes.

LEIGH ANSLEY CATERING

THYME SAVER

Before you pour sticky substances into a measuring cup, spray the cup lightly with nonstick cooking spray. Watch how easily your honey or peanut butter comes right out.

Almond Blueberry Coffee Cake

7 ounces almond paste, chilled

1 pint blueberries, rinsed

2 tablespoons all-purpose flour

2 teaspoons grated lemon zest

2 cups all-purpose flour

2 teaspoons baking powder

1/2 teaspoon baking soda

1/4 teaspoon salt

3/4 cup (1 1/2 sticks) butter, softened

1 1/4 cups granulated sugar

2 eggs

1 teaspoon vanilla extract

1 cup sour cream

2 tablespoons confectioners' sugar

Preheat the oven to 350 degrees. Grease and flour a 10-inch bundt pan. (If a coated bundt pan is being used, just spray with nonstick cooking spray.) Grate the almond paste into a medium bowl. Add the blueberries, 2 tablespoons flour and the lemon zest and mix well. Sift 2 cups flour, the baking powder, baking soda and salt together.

Beat the butter and granulated sugar in a mixing bowl until smooth and creamy. Add the eggs one at a time, beating well after each addition. Scrape down the side of the bowl and beat until light and fluffy. Beat in the vanilla. Add the flour mixture and sour cream alternately, beating constantly and beginning and ending with the flour mixture.

Layer one-third of the batter, one-half of the blueberry mixture, one-half of the remaining batter, remaining blueberry mixture and remaining batter in the prepared bundt pan. Bake for 45 minutes or until the cake is deep golden brown and a wooden pick inserted near the center comes out clean. Cool in the pan on a wire rack for 20 minutes. Loosen the cake from the side of the pan gently with a thin spatula. Invert onto a wire rack to cool completely. Sprinkle with the confectioners' sugar.

CINDY WISE

LIGHTEN UP

When trying to improve the nutritional profile of a recipe, an ingredient can be eliminated, substituted, or reduced. This recipe could be nutritionally improved by reducing the butter and granulated sugar and by substituting reduced-fat or fat-free sour cream. However, there are recipes that speak to tradition. If this or another recipe is one of those family favorites, enjoy it as is; just do so occasionally.

Praline Brunch Toast

8 eggs
1 1/2 cups half-and-half
1 tablespoon light brown sugar
2 teaspoons vanilla extract
8 (3/4-inch-thick) slices
  sourdough bread
1/4 cup (1/2 stick) butter
3/4 cup packed light brown sugar
1/2 cup maple syrup
1/2 teaspoon cinnamon
3/4 cup chopped pecans
1/4 cup confectioners' sugar

Preheat the oven to 300 degrees. Beat the eggs, half-and-half, 1 tablespoon brown sugar and the vanilla in a bowl. Pour one-half of the mixture into a 9×13-inch baking pan. Arrange the bread tightly in one layer over the egg mixture, trimming the slices to fit if necessary. Pour the remaining egg mixture over the bread. Chill, covered, for 8 to 10 hours.

Microwave the butter on High for 1 minute in a large microwave-safe dish. Add 3/4 cup brown sugar, the maple syrup and cinnamon. Stir in the pecans. Pour evenly over the soaked bread. Bake, uncovered, for 30 to 35 minutes or until golden brown. Let stand for 2 to 5 minutes. Sprinkle with the confectioners' sugar and serve immediately.

ORIGINALLY PUBLISHED IN *Finding Thyme*

Bananas Foster Bread

1/4 cup sugar
1/4 teaspoon cinnamon
1 tablespoon butter
3 very ripe bananas
1/4 cup (1/2 stick) butter, melted
1/2 teaspoon baking soda
1 1/2 cups whole wheat flour
3/4 cup honey
1/2 cup cinnamon chips
1/2 cup walnuts or pecans

Preheat the oven to 350 degrees. Mix the sugar and cinnamon in a bowl. Grease a 5×7-inch loaf pan with 1 tablespoon butter. Coat the pan with the cinnamon-sugar. Mash the bananas with a fork in a bowl. Stir in 1/4 cup butter, the baking soda, flour, honey, cinnamon chips and walnuts. Pour into the prepared pan. Bake for 1 hour or until a wooden pick inserted in the center comes out clean.

AMANDA PORTER

Cinnamon Snails

4 slices soft texture whole wheat
  bread or white bread
1/4 cup tub-style cream cheese
3 tablespoons sugar
1 1/2 teaspoons cinnamon
1/4 cup (1/2 stick) butter, melted

Preheat the oven to 350 degrees. Trim the crusts from the bread. Spread 1 tablespoon of the cream cheese over each bread slice and roll up. Cut each roll-up into thirds. Mix the sugar and cinnamon in a bowl. Brush each roll with the melted butter and roll in the cinnamon-sugar. Do not brush the butter over the ends of the rolls. Place rolls seam side down on an ungreased baking sheet. Bake for 12 minutes or until light brown and crisp. Serve warm or cool.

AMANDA PORTER

Cranberry Walnut Bread

BREAD
2 cups all-purpose flour
1 cup sugar
2 teaspoons baking powder
1/2 teaspoon baking soda
1 teaspoon salt
2 teaspoons orange zest
1/3 cup orange juice
1/2 cup water
1 egg, beaten
2 tablespoons vegetable oil
1 cup fresh cranberries, chopped
1 cup chopped walnuts

CRANBERRY BUTTER
1 cup (2 sticks) butter, softened
1/2 cup dried cranberries
1/2 teaspoon cinnamon

To prepare the bread, preheat the oven to 350 degrees. Sift the flour, sugar, baking powder, baking soda and salt together in a large bowl. Combine the orange zest, orange juice, water, egg and oil in a large bowl and mix well. Add the flour mixture and stir until moistened. Stir in the cranberries and walnuts. Pour into 1 large or 2 small nonstick loaf pans. Bake for 1 hour and 15 minutes or until a wooden pick inserted in the center comes out clean.

To prepare the butter, process the butter, cranberries and cinnamon in a food processor. Spoon into a small bowl. Serve with the bread.

For variation, substitute 1/4 cup each chopped almonds, chopped walnuts, chopped pecans and chopped hazelnuts for the walnuts.

Zucchini Nut Bread

SERVES 10 TO 12

2 cups sifted all-purpose flour
1 teaspoon cinnamon
1/2 teaspoon baking soda
1/2 teaspoon salt
1/4 teaspoon baking powder
2 eggs
1 1/3 cups sugar
2/3 cup vegetable oil
2 teaspoons vanilla extract
1 1/3 cups shredded zucchini
1/2 cup chopped nuts

Preheat the oven to 350 degrees. Sift the flour, cinnamon, baking soda, salt and baking powder together. Beat the eggs at medium speed in a mixing bowl until blended. Add the sugar and oil gradually, mixing well after each addition. Stir in the vanilla. Add the flour mixture and beat at low speed until blended. Stir in the zucchini and nuts. Pour into a greased 5×9-inch loaf pan. Bake for 1 hour to 1 hour and 15 minutes or until a tester inserted in the center comes out clean. Let cool in the pan on a wire rack for 10 minutes.

MEGAN HENSLEY

Pumpkin Muffins

MAKES 24

3 1/2 cups all-purpose flour
2 1/2 cups sugar
2 teaspoons baking soda
1 1/2 teaspoons salt
1 teaspoon cinnamon
1 teaspoon nutmeg
1 (15-ounce) can pumpkin
1 cup canola oil
4 eggs
Cream Cheese Frosting
   (page 151)

Preheat the oven to 350 degrees. Mix the flour, sugar, baking soda, salt, cinnamon and nutmeg in a large bowl. Combine the pumpkin and canola oil in a medium bowl and mix well. Add the eggs one at a time, beating well after each addition. Make a well in the center of the flour mixture. Add the pumpkin mixture and stir until the flour mixture is moistened. Spoon about 1/4 cup of the batter into each paper-lined muffin cup. Bake for 20 to 25 minutes or until brown. Let cool on a wire rack. Spread with the frosting.

ROBYN BROCK

LIGHTEN UP

The 1 cup of oil alone in these muffins provides 36 grams of fat and 318 calories per serving. When baking, oil can almost always be reduced by one-fourth to one-third without the need to add anything else to the recipe. Even more can be cut by adding a liquid like water, fruit juice, or skim milk to make up for some of the moisture loss. In this recipe, if applesauce is used for at least one-half of the oil and egg substitute is used in place of the eggs, the fat will plummet to 6 grams per serving, offering a significantly better nutritional picture.

Ap·pe·tiz·ers

(ap'·ĭ tī'·zers)

1. Savory bites served to stimulate

the appetite.

Feta Black Bean Dip

SERVES 30

1/2 cup sugar
3/4 cup apple cider vinegar
3/4 cup vegetable oil
3 (15-ounce) cans black beans,
  drained and rinsed
3 (15-ounce) cans Shoe Peg corn,
  drained and rinsed
1 bunch scallions, chopped
1 bunch cilantro, chopped
1 (8-ounce) block feta cheese,
  crumbled

Whisk the sugar, vinegar and oil in a large bowl. Add the black beans, corn, scallions, cilantro and cheese and mix well. Chill until serving time. Serve with tortilla chips or corn chips.

Photograph for this recipe appears on page 22.

Baked Crab Rangoon

SERVES 6

6 ounces fresh jumbo lump crab
  meat, drained and flaked
4 ounces cream cheese, softened
1/4 cup thinly sliced scallions
1/4 cup mayonnaise
12 miniature frozen phyllo shells
Chopped scallions for garnish

Preheat the oven to 350 degrees. Mix the crab meat, cream cheese, 1/4 cup scallions and the mayonnaise in a medium bowl. Place the phyllo shells on a baking sheet. Fill evenly with the crab meat mixture. Bake for 18 to 20 minutes or until the filling is heated through. Garnish with chopped scallions. Serve warm.

THYME SAVER

Deciding how many appetizers you need for a party is often difficult. Many caterers use this rule of thumb: Twelve appetizers per person should be enough for a cocktail party and six per person will do for a dinner party. Having an equal number of hot and cold foods is helpful so that while one appetizer is heating in the oven, a cold one can be circulating, keeping everyone nibbling.

Mussels Marinara

1/3 cup extra-virgin olive oil
4 garlic cloves, finely chopped
1 (28-ounce) can crushed tomatoes
1 cup white wine
3 pounds mussels, scrubbed and
  debearded
1 teaspoon salt
1/2 teaspoon crushed red pepper
2 tablespoons fresh parsley, finely
  chopped
1 loaf crusty French bread

Heat the olive oil in a large saucepan over medium heat. Add the garlic and sauté for 5 minutes or until soft. Add the tomatoes and wine. Cook, uncovered, for 10 minutes. Add the mussels, salt and red pepper. Cook, tightly covered, for 7 minutes or until the mussel shells open. Pour into a serving bowl and sprinkle with the parsley. Serve with the bread, which is great for dipping in the sauce.

Serve over linguine for an entrée.

MICHAEL COLLEY

Tangy Bacon-Wrapped Shrimp

2 pounds extra-large shrimp,
  peeled and deveined
2 cups Mojo liquid marinade
1 pound bacon, cut into
  3-inch strips
2 cups finely chopped scallions
2 lemons, cut into halves
2 lemons, cut into wedges
1/2 cup (1 stick) butter, clarified
1 tablespoon lemon juice

Place the shrimp in a 1-gallon sealable plastic freezer bag. Add the marinade and seal the bag. Shake until the shrimp are evenly coated. Marinate in the refrigerator for 1 hour. Drain the shrimp, discarding the marinade. Wrap each shrimp with a slice of bacon and secure with a wooden pick. Place on a rack in a broiler pan. Sprinkle with the scallions. Squeeze the juice from the lemon halves over the shrimp. Broil for 2 minutes. Turn over and broil for 2 minutes longer or until the shrimp turn pink. Garnish with the lemon wedges. Mix the clarified butter with 1 tablespoon lemon juice in a bowl. Serve with the shrimp.

JIM MAGILL

Sweet-and-Sour Meatballs

SWEET-AND-SOUR SAUCE
2 (12-ounce) bottles chili sauce
2 cups tomato juice
1 cup water
1 cup dark corn syrup
1/4 cup fresh lemon juice
1 to 2 tablespoons chili powder
2 tablespoons dried oregano
1/4 teaspoon garlic salt
1/2 teaspoon Tabasco sauce
3 tablespoons brown sugar

MEATBALLS
3 pounds ground beef
4 eggs
2 onions, finely chopped
1 1/4 cups dry bread crumbs
2 teaspoons chili powder
1 tablespoon salt
1 teaspoon garlic salt
1 teaspoon freshly ground pepper
2 to 3 tablespoons vegetable oil

To prepare the sauce, combine the chili sauce, tomato juice, water, corn syrup, lemon juice, chili powder, oregano, garlic salt, Tabasco sauce and brown sugar in a bowl and mix well.

To prepare the meatballs, combine the ground beef, eggs, onions, bread crumbs, chili powder, salt, garlic salt, pepper and oil in a large bowl and mix well. Shape into small meatballs. Sauté in a skillet until cooked through. Pour the sauce evenly over the meatballs and cook until heated through. Spoon into a chafing dish or a slow cooker set on Low to keep warm.

To serve as an entrée, shape the ground beef mixture into larger balls and serve over thick egg noodles for a fun twist on stroganoff.

SALLY KARIOTH

Sausage Delights

2 cups (8 ounces) extra-sharp
  Cheddar cheese, shredded
1 pound hot or mild bulk
  pork sausage
2 tablespoons Worcestershire
  sauce
1 tablespoon milk
1/2 teaspoon Tabasco sauce
1 1/2 cups Bisquick

Preheat the oven to 400 degrees. Combine the cheese, sausage, Worcestershire sauce, milk, Tabasco sauce and baking mix in a bowl and mix well. Shape into 1-inch balls and place 1 inch apart on a greased baking sheet. Bake for 10 to 15 minutes or until brown. Serve hot.

To prepare in advance, freeze the uncooked sausage balls for up to 1 week. When ready to use, remove from the freezer and bake as directed above.

BETSY CAIRE COUCH

Bruschetta

6 plum tomatoes, cut into
  halves lengthwise
2 tablespoons extra-virgin
  olive oil
Salt and pepper to taste
7 garlic cloves
4 kalamata olives, pitted
  and chopped
2 tablespoons finely sliced
  fresh mint
1 loaf French bread, cut into
  1/4-inch-thick slices
Extra-virgin olive oil for brushing

Preheat the oven to 350 degrees. Arrange the tomatoes cut side up in a single layer in a shallow baking dish. Drizzle with 2 tablespoons olive oil and sprinkle with salt and pepper. Place the garlic around the tomatoes.

Roast on the middle oven rack for 1 hour or until the tomatoes are tender and the skins are wrinkled. Remove from the oven to cool. Remove the tomatoes to a chopping board, reserving the garlic and oil in the baking dish. Chop the tomatoes. Combine the tomatoes, olives and mint in a bowl and mix well.

Brush the bread lightly on both sides with olive oil and place on a baking sheet. Bake for 15 minutes or until golden brown. Peel the reserved roasted garlic cloves. Mash the garlic cloves in a bowl to form a paste. Add the reserved oil and mix well. Spread on the toasted bread slices and top with the tomato mixture.

The tomatoes and garlic paste can be prepared one day ahead and chilled, covered, in the refrigerator. Bring to room temperature before proceeding. The toast can be prepared one day ahead and kept in an airtight container at room temperature. To serve, assemble and bake in a preheated 350-degree oven.

ORIGINALLY PUBLISHED IN *Finding Thyme*

LIGHTEN UP

Often appetizers boost calories and fat but not necessarily nutrients. Including an appetizer with vegetables as the major ingredients in a recipe can boost important nutrients and add delicious flavor. Promote a healthy diet by including a menu full of fruits and vegetables.

Artichoke Bites

SERVES 8

1 (8-ounce) can artichoke hearts, drained and finely chopped
1 cup (4 ounces) shredded Cheddar cheese
3/4 cup mayonnaise
1/2 envelope Italian salad dressing mix
1/4 cup (1 ounce) grated Parmesan cheese
1 Boboli pizza crust

Preheat the oven to 400 degrees. Combine the artichoke hearts, Cheddar cheese, mayonnaise, salad dressing mix and Parmesan cheese in a medium bowl and mix well. Spread over the pizza shell. Bake for 15 to 20 minutes or until hot and bubbly. Let cool and cut into bite-size pieces.

NORMA BARTEK

Wine-Infused Mushrooms

SERVES 4 TO 6

1 pound mushrooms
1/4 cup chopped onion
1/4 cup chopped celery
1/4 cup (1/2 stick) butter
1 teaspoon Worcestershire sauce
1/2 teaspoon salt
1/8 teaspoon pepper
1/4 cup white wine
1/4 cup bread crumbs
1 1/2 tablespoons grated Parmesan cheese
Melted butter for brushing
1/4 cup (1 ounce) shredded mozzarella cheese or Cheddar cheese

Preheat the oven to 350 degrees. Clean the mushrooms with damp paper towels. Remove the stems, reserving the caps. Finely chop the stems. Sauté the onion, celery and mushroom stems in 1/4 cup butter in a skillet until the celery is tender. Stir in the Worcestershire sauce, salt, pepper, wine, bread crumbs and Parmesan cheese. Brush the reserved mushroom caps with melted butter and fill with the vegetable mixture. Arrange in a greased shallow baking dish. Sprinkle with the mozzarella cheese. Bake for 15 minutes or until the cheese melts.

BOO HARTSELL

Olive Muffin Puffs

6 English muffins
1/2 cup black olives
1/2 cup green olives
1/2 cup sliced scallions
1 1/2 cups (6 ounces) shredded
   sharp Cheddar cheese
1/2 cup mayonnaise
1/2 teaspoon salt
1/2 teaspoon curry powder

Preheat the oven to 350 degrees. Place the English muffins on a baking sheet. Bake for 7 minutes or until toasted. Split the English muffins and cut into quarters. Pulse the olives in a food processor until finely chopped. Combine the olives, scallions, cheese, mayonnaise, salt and curry powder in a bowl and mix well. Spoon 1 heaping tablespoon of the olive mixture onto each muffin quarter and place on a baking sheet. Place on the bottom oven rack. Broil for 3 to 5 minutes or until the cheese melts. For variation, add 1 cup fresh lump crab meat. The topping can be made in advance and then assembled and broiled just before serving.

LORI B. MATTICE

Almond-Encrusted Brie with Cranberry Chutney

CRANBERRY CHUTNEY
1/4 cup granulated sugar
1/4 cup packed brown sugar
1/2 cup cider vinegar
1/4 cup dried cranberries
1/2 teaspoon orange zest
1/4 cup chopped walnuts

BRIE CHEESE
2 cups peanut oil
3/4 cup all-purpose flour
2 eggs
1/2 teaspoon salt
1/2 teaspoon pepper
1/4 cup ground almonds
1/4 cup panko (Japanese
   bread crumbs)
4 wedges Brie cheese with rind
Mixed baby greens or spring
   lettuce mix
Thinly sliced oranges for garnish

To prepare the chutney, combine the granulated sugar, brown sugar and vinegar in a small saucepan and mix well. Bring to a high simmer. Simmer for 15 minutes or until the mixture is thick and reduced by one-half. Stir in the cranberries, orange zest and walnuts. Remove from the heat and let stand at room temperature.

To prepare the Brie cheese, heat the peanut oil in a saucepan over medium heat. Place the flour in a small bowl. Beat the eggs with the salt and pepper in a bowl. Mix the almonds and panko in a bowl. Coat the Brie cheese with the flour, dip in the egg mixture and then coat with the panko mixture. Fry in the hot peanut oil for 1 1/2 minutes. Remove to paper towels to drain.

To serve, place the Brie cheese on a bed of mixed baby greens and spoon the chutney over the top. Garnish with orange slices.

SUZANNE HUGHES

Brandy Pecan Brie

1/4 cup pecans
1/4 cup packed brown sugar
1 tablespoon brandy
1 wheel Brie cheese
2 pears, sliced
2 green apples, sliced
Assorted crackers

Preheat the oven to 500 degrees. Pulse the pecans and brown sugar in a food processor until finely ground. Spoon into a bowl and stir in the brandy. Place the Brie cheese on a baking sheet. Bake for 5 minutes or until lightly browned on top and soft. Place on a serving plate. Spoon the brown sugar topping over the Brie cheese. Surround with the pears, apples and crackers for serving. Serve immediately.

ELAINE DRABIK

Brie Kisses

1/3 pound Brie cheese
1 (17-ounce) package frozen
   puff pastry
1 (10-ounce) jar red and green
   hot pepper jelly

Preheat the oven to 400 degrees. Cut the Brie cheese into thirty-two 1/2-inch cubes. Arrange on a plate and place in the freezer. Thaw the pastry for 40 minutes or thaw using the package directions.

Unfold each pastry sheet and roll with a rolling pin to remove the creases. Cut each sheet into quarters. Cut each quarter into halves. Cut each half into halves to produce a total of 32 squares. Place the squares into greased miniature muffin cups so the corners point upwards. Bake for 5 minutes.

Place one frozen Brie cheese cube in the center of each pastry. Bake for 10 minutes or until the edges are golden brown. Remove from the muffin cups and immediately top with the pepper jelly.

For variation, substitute a slice of pear, apple or olive for the pepper jelly.

BOO HARTSELL

Beefy Cheese Ball

SERVES 50

8 ounces cream cheese, softened
1 (3-ounce) package dried
  beef, chopped
1/2 large onion, chopped
2 cups (8 ounces) shredded
  Cheddar cheese

Combine the cream cheese, dried beef, onion and Cheddar cheese in a mixing bowl and beat well. Shape into a ball and place on a serving plate. Serve with butter crackers. You may prepare the cheese ball in advance and store, covered, in the refrigerator until ready to serve.

MELISSA K. JOINER

Sun-Dried Tomato Pesto

SERVES 6 TO 8

1 sourdough baguette
1 (8-ounce) jar julienned
  sun-dried tomatoes in olive oil
1 cup fresh basil
2 garlic cloves
3/4 cup (3 ounces) freshly grated
  Parmesan cheese
3 tablespoons extra-virgin
  olive oil
1/2 teaspoon dried thyme
1/2 teaspoon dried rosemary
8 ounces cream cheese, softened

Preheat the oven to 350 degrees. Cut the baguette into 2-inch slices and arrange on a baking sheet. Bake until hot and crispy. Pulse the sun-dried tomatoes, basil, garlic, Parmesan cheese, olive oil, thyme, rosemary and cream cheese in a food processor until well blended. Spread evenly over the hot bread. Bake for a few minutes or until the topping melts slightly. Serve warm.

For variation, you may bake the topping separately at 350 degrees until warm and bubbly and serve with crackers or toasted bread slices.

KATE JOHNSTON

TALLAHASSEE TIDBIT

The first Christmas Mass celebrated in the United States was held in Tallahassee during the 1539–1540 encampment of Spanish explorer Hernando de Soto. The site of de Soto's encampment was discovered in 1987 on Tallahassee's east side and remains the only archaeological evidence of de Soto's expedition in North America.

Sausage Feta Spread

SERVES 8

1 pound Italian sausage,
  casings removed
1 loaf French bread
2 tablespoons extra-virgin
  olive oil
4 garlic cloves, minced
2 cups chopped plum tomatoes or
  cherry tomatoes
Salt and pepper to taste
1 (8-ounce) package crumbled
  feta cheese
1 teaspoon fresh basil
1 (4-ounce) can sliced black
  olives, drained

Preheat the oven to 350 degrees. Brown the Italian sausage in a skillet over medium-high heat. Remove from the heat to cool. Cut the bread into 1/2-inch rounds and place on a baking sheet. Bake for 10 minutes or until lightly toasted. Remove from the oven to cool.

Heat the olive oil in a medium saucepan over medium-high heat. Add the garlic and sauté for 2 minutes. Add the tomatoes, salt and pepper. Cook for 5 minutes. Mix the cheese and basil in a small bowl. Add the hot tomato mixture and stir until the cheese melts. Add the olives and sausage and mix well. Spread on the toasted bread slices and serve immediately.

MARGARET HOLGATE

Crunchy Olive Spread

SERVES 4 TO 8

6 ounces cream cheese, softened
1/2 cup mayonnaise
1/2 cup chopped pecans
1 cup chopped manzanilla olives
  with pimento
1/8 teaspoon freshly ground pepper

Combine the cream cheese and mayonnaise in a bowl and mix well. Add the pecans, olives and pepper and mix well. Chill, covered, for 24 to 48 hours. Serve with crackers or toast points.

VERA PETERSEN

Raspberry Cheese Spread

SERVES 12 TO 16

4 cups (16 ounces) sharp
  Cheddar cheese, shredded
1 cup pecans, finely chopped
1 cup finely chopped onion
1 cup mayonnaise
1 (12-ounce) jar seedless red
  raspberry jam

Combine the cheese, pecans and onion in a bowl. Add the mayonnaise and mix well. Chill until serving time. To serve, invert the cheese mixture onto a platter and shape into a ball. Pour the jam over the ball or press an indention in the center of the ball and fill to overflowing with the jam. Serve with butter crackers.

ORIGINALLY PUBLISHED IN *Thymes Remembered*

Mexican Lasagna Dip

SERVES 15

1 pound ground beef
1 cup chopped onion
2 (16-ounce) cans refried beans
2 (4-ounce) cans green chiles
1 (16-ounce) jar salsa
1 (4-ounce) can sliced black
  olives, drained
1/4 cup chopped jalapeño chiles
16 ounces cream cheese,
  cut into slices
2 cups (8 ounces) shredded
  Mexican cheese blend

Preheat the oven to 400 degrees. Brown the ground beef with the onion in a large skillet, stirring until the ground beef is crumbly; drain. Stir in the refried beans, green chiles, salsa, olives and jalapeño chiles. Pour into a 9×13-inch glass baking dish. Layer the cream cheese and Mexican cheese over the top. Bake for 15 minutes or until brown and bubbly. Serve with blue corn tortilla chips.

ANITA CROCKETT

LIGHTEN UP

With many dips, the dipper is a huge calorie and fat culprit. Bake your own corn chips or avoid the full-fat regular chips by purchasing the baked version of your favorite. Target the cream cheese, refried beans, olives, and Mexican cheese to reduce the additional fat in this recipe. An easy remedy is to use reduced-fat cream cheese and Mexican cheese, use fat-free refried beans, and eliminate the olives.

Smoked Mullet Dip

1 medium piece of smoked mullet
16 ounces cottage cheese
1 envelope ranch salad
   dressing mix

Remove the bones and skin from the fish. Flake the fish. Process the fish, cottage cheese and salad dressing mix in a blender until well mixed. Pour into a serving bowl. Chill, covered, in the refrigerator. Serve cold with your favorite chips or crackers.

DR. T. K. AND VIRGINIA WETHERELL

Pastrami Bread Dip

8 ounces cream cheese
7 ounces shaved pastrami
4 cups (16 ounces) shredded
   Cheddar cheese
1/2 bell pepper, chopped
1 bunch scallions, chopped
1 tomato, chopped
1/4 teaspoon chili powder
1/2 teaspoon hot red pepper sauce
1 loaf Italian or French bread

Preheat the oven to 350 degrees. Place the cream cheese in a medium or large microwave-safe bowl. Microwave on High at 30-second intervals until the cream cheese is softened. Add the pastrami, Cheddar cheese, bell pepper, scallions, tomato, chili powder and hot sauce and mix well.

Hollow out the bread and fill evenly with the pastrami mixture. Place on a baking sheet. Bake for 30 minutes or until heated through. Serve warm with corn chips.

BROOKE SPICER

Creamy Artichoke Dip

SERVES 12

1 wedge Parmesan cheese
1 garlic clove, minced
8 ounces cream cheese, softened
2 tablespoons mayonnaise
1 (14-ounce) can water-pack
   artichokes, drained
   and chopped

Preheat the oven to 325 degrees. Grate the Parmesan cheese in a food processor. Combine the Parmesan cheese, garlic, cream cheese, mayonnaise and artichokes in a bowl and mix well. Spoon into an oven-proof serving dish. Bake for 20 to 30 minutes or until heated through. Serve with tortilla chips or corn chips.

This dip also may be used as a spread. Serve with sliced French bread.

HESTER COWLES NDOJA

The Perfect Corn Dip

SERVES 8 TO 10

2 (8-ounce) cans Mexicorn,
   drained
1 (10-ounce) can tomatoes with
   green chiles, drained
1/2 cup chopped scallions
2 cups (8 ounces) shredded
   Cheddar cheese
1/2 cup mayonnaise
1/2 cup sour cream
Salt and pepper to taste

Combine the Mexicorn, tomatoes with green chiles, scallions, cheese, mayonnaise, sour cream, salt and pepper in a bowl and mix well. Chill, covered, for 1 to 10 hours. Serve with corn chips or tortilla chips. This dip tastes best if prepared the night before.

CAROLE STRANGE

LIGHTEN UP

Appetizers and munchies are both welcoming and irresistible. This recipe can be lightened by choosing reduced-fat mayonnaise, reduced-fat sour cream, and baked chips for a big savings of calories and fat.

Hot Savory Dip

1 (10-ounce) package frozen
   seasoning blend
24 ounces cream cheese, softened
1/2 cup mayonnaise
1 teaspoon garlic powder
2 1/2 cups (10 ounces) grated
   Parmesan cheese
Dash of parsley flakes

Preheat the oven to 350 degrees. Thaw the seasoning blend and pat dry. Combine the cream cheese, mayonnaise and garlic powder in a bowl and mix well. Add the seasoning blend and mix well. Stir in the Parmesan cheese. Spoon into a greased 9×9-inch baking dish. Sprinkle with parsley flakes. Bake for 30 minutes or until light brown.

SUSAN VAN LEUVEN

Sizzlin' Salsa

1 (15-ounce) can black beans,
   drained and rinsed
1 (15-ounce) can black-eyed
   peas, drained and rinsed
1 (15-ounce) can Shoe Peg corn,
   drained and rinsed
1 (10-ounce) can diced tomatoes
   with green chiles, drained
3 Roma tomatoes, chopped
1 green bell pepper, chopped
1 green onion, finely chopped
3/4 (16-ounce) bottle zesty Italian
   salad dressing

Combine the black beans, black-eyed peas, corn, tomatoes with green chiles, tomatoes, bell pepper and green onion in a bowl and mix well. Add the salad dressing and mix well. Serve with tortilla chips. The salsa is best if chilled for 4 hours before serving. It may be stored in the refrigerator for up to 3 days.

PEP CULPEPPER

THYME SAVER

Don't throw away the rind of Parmigiano-Reggiano or Romano cheese; use it to flavor and thicken stocks, soups, and stews. Freeze leftover rinds and add them to enhance your favorite soup recipes. Just remember to remove the rind before serving.

Grilled Pineapple Salsa

2 slices fresh pineapple, grilled
  and chopped
2 cups blanched
  chopped asparagus
1 cup chopped red onion
2 cups chopped, seeded and
  peeled tomatoes
1/2 cup semi-dried
  tomatoes, chopped
1/4 cup fresh basil, chopped
1/4 cup fresh chives, chopped
1/4 cup fresh parsley, chopped
1/4 cup olive oil
1/4 cup balsamic vinegar
Salt and pepper to taste
1 (16-ounce) package pita bread
1 garlic clove

Preheat the oven to 350 degrees. Combine the pineapple, asparagus, onion, tomatoes, herbs, olive oil, vinegar, salt and pepper in a bowl and mix well. Let stand at room temperature for 1 hour. Rub the pita bread lightly with the garlic clove and place on a baking sheet. Bake until lightly toasted. Cut into wedges. Dip into the salsa and use as a scoop. As an alternative, you may use garlic-flavored pita bread.

PHYLLIS STEPHENS

Balsamic Strawberry Salsa

MAKES 6 CUPS

2 tablespoons extra-virgin
  olive oil
2 tablespoons balsamic vinegar
1 teaspoon salt
1 pint fresh strawberries,
  coarsely chopped
8 scallions, chopped
2 pints cherry tomatoes, seeded
  and chopped
1/2 cup chopped fresh cilantro
1/2 lime

Process the olive oil, vinegar and salt in a blender until well mixed. Mix the strawberries, scallions, tomatoes and cilantro in a medium bowl. Squeeze the juice from the lime over the mixture and toss to mix. Add the vinaigrette and toss to coat. Chill for 4 hours or longer. Serve with tortilla chips.

LILY ETEMADI

Soups & Sal·ads

[soops] & [sal·uh·ds]

1. Liquid food for warming the soul.

2. Crisp dish consisting of fresh garden

vegetables or fruit.

Tomato Bisque

6 tablespoons unsalted butter

1/2 cup chopped onion

5 cups chopped, peeled and seeded Fresh Florida sun-ripe tomatoes

4 cups chicken stock

2 tablespoons unsalted butter

2 tablespoons all-purpose flour

2 teaspoons salt

1/2 teaspoon white pepper

1/4 cup chopped fresh parsley

1 1/2 teaspoons fresh chopped basil

1 tablespoon smoked paprika

1 1/4 cups heavy cream

2/3 cup half-and-half

Melt 6 tablespoons butter in a large saucepan over medium heat. Add the onion. Cook for 5 minutes or until the onion is translucent. Add the tomatoes and stock. Bring to a simmer.

Melt 2 tablespoons butter in a small saucepan over medium heat. Whisk in the flour to form a roux. Cook for 3 minutes, whisking constantly. Do not brown. Whisk the roux into the stock mixture until well mixed. Add the salt and white pepper. Bring to a boil, stirring occasionally. Reduce the heat.

Simmer for 15 minutes. Stir in the parsley, basil, paprika, cream and half-and-half. Remove from the heat. Purée with an immersion blender. Strain before serving, if desired. Ladle into soup bowls. Serve with a few slices of wheat bread.

CHEF JOSH BUTLER, FLORIDA GOVERNOR'S MANSION

Photograph for this recipe appears on page 38.

TALLAHASSEE TIDBIT

Florida's 44th governor, Charlie Crist, was born in 1956 in Altoona, Pennsylvania, but his family soon settled in St. Petersburg. As a public school student, Governor Crist quickly learned the value of participation, leading him to serve as class president at St. Petersburg High School and, later, as student body vice-president at Florida State University. The Tomato Bisque is Governor Crist's favorite soup.

Sweet Pepper Shrimp Bisque

SERVES 6

1 tablespoon extra-virgin olive oil
1 red bell pepper, chopped
1 cup chopped yellow onion
1/2 cup uncooked shrimp,
    tails removed and shrimp
    cut into pieces
2 cups half-and-half
1 cup no-salt-added tomato sauce
1/4 teaspoon hot red pepper
    sauce, or to taste
Salt and pepper to taste
1 teaspoon butter
1/4 cup (1 ounce) freshly grated
    Parmesan cheese

Heat the olive oil in a saucepan. Add the bell pepper and onion. Cook over low heat until soft, stirring occasionally. Add the shrimp, half-and-half, tomato sauce, hot sauce, salt and pepper. Bring to a boil and reduce the heat. Simmer for 5 minutes. Add the butter. Process carefully one-half at a time at high speed in a blender for 10 to 15 seconds. Pour into soup bowls. Sprinkle with the cheese.

KITTY BALL

Butternut Bisque

SERVES 6 TO 8

5 pounds butternut squash,
    peeled and chopped
5 cups chicken stock
2 cups heavy cream
3 cups light cream
1 chicken bouillon cube
1/4 cup maple syrup
1/2 teaspoon white pepper

Combine the squash and stock in a stockpot. Simmer, covered, until the squash is tender. Blend in a blender or food processor until smooth. Return to the stockpot. Add the heavy cream, light cream, bouillon cube, maple syrup and white pepper and mix well. Heat slowly until slightly thickened, stirring frequently. Do not boil. Ladle into soup bowls. Serve warm.

ORIGINALLY PUBLISHED IN *Finding Thyme*

LIGHTEN UP
Enhance the richness of this soup and keep fat to a minimum by using evaporated skim milk instead of cream. If making such a change seems too drastic but reducing fat is still desired, start slowly. Reduce up to half the cream with a lower-fat choice to gain confidence and ensure your enjoyment of the final dish.

Crab and Corn Bisque

1/2 cup chopped celery
1/2 cup chopped scallions
1/2 cup chopped green
   bell pepper
1/4 cup (1/2 stick) butter
2 (10-ounce) cans cream of
   potato soup
1 (14-ounce) can cream-style corn
1 1/2 cups half-and-half
1 1/2 cups milk
2 bay leaves
1 tablespoon fresh thyme, or
   1/2 to 1 teaspoon dried thyme
3/4 teaspoon white pepper
1/8 teaspoon hot red pepper sauce
1 pound fresh lump crab meat
Chopped fresh parsley or chives
   for garnish

Sauté the celery, scallions and bell pepper in the butter in a Dutch oven over medium heat until tender. Add the soup, corn, half-and-half, milk, bay leaves, thyme, white pepper and hot sauce. Cook until heated through. Stir in the crab meat gently. Cook until heated through. Discard the bay leaves. Ladle into soup bowls. Garnish with chopped fresh parsley.

REPRESENTATIVE ALAN WILLIAMS'S AUNT JEAN

TALLAHASSEE TIDBIT

Lifelong Tallahassean State Representative Alan Williams has been politically and philanthropically active since he was a student at Florida A&M University. During the 2008 presidential election, Alan served as the master of ceremonies to both President Barack Obama's rallies in Tallahassee. Alan attributes this recipe to his Aunt Jean, an educator and Florida A&M University graduate, who serves this bisque as a Thanksgiving tradition.

Chicken and Andouille Gumbo

4 pounds skinned and boned
  chicken thighs
1 pound andouille sausage,
  casings removed
1 cup vegetable oil
1 cup all-purpose flour
4 onions, minced
2 green bell peppers, chopped
2 large ribs celery, chopped
4 garlic cloves, minced
8 cups chicken broth
1 1/2 teaspoons dried thyme
1/2 teaspoon red pepper
1 tablespoon Worcestershire sauce
1/3 cup fresh parsley
Tabasco sauce to taste
Hot cooked rice

Preheat the oven to 350 degrees. Place the chicken in a baking pan. Bake for 40 minutes, turning after 20 minutes. Brown the sausage in a large skillet, stirring until crumbly. Remove from the skillet and drain. Wipe out the skillet with a paper towel.

Place the oil and flour in the skillet. Cook over medium heat for 25 minutes or until the roux turns mahogany in color, whisking constantly. Add the onions, bell peppers, celery and garlic. Cook for 20 minutes or until the vegetables are tender, stirring frequently. Add the broth gradually. Add the thyme and red pepper.

Cut the chicken into bite-size pieces. Stir the chicken, sausage and Worcestershire sauce into the vegetable mixture. Bring to a boil over medium-high heat and reduce the heat. Simmer for 2 1/2 to 3 hours, stirring occasionally. Add the parsley and Tabasco sauce just before serving. Remove from the heat. Ladle over rice in soup bowls.

DR. MICHAEL CAIRE

Cambo Gumbo

4 slices bacon

1 onion, or 2 bunches
 scallions, chopped

2 garlic cloves, minced

1 (16-ounce) package frozen
 chopped okra

Small amount of all-purpose flour

2 cups hot beef broth

Ham broth or ham bouillon

1/2 to 2 cups hot and spicy
 vegetable juice cocktail

2 to 3 cups chopped
 peeled tomatoes

1/4 cup fresh parsley, minced

1 tablespoon Tabasco sauce

1 tablespoon Worcestershire sauce

Few strands of saffron

Salt, garlic salt and pepper
 to taste

1 to 1 1/2 pounds fresh shrimp,
 peeled and cut into halves

8 to 16 ounces grouper fillet,
 fingers or cheeks, cut into
 1- to 1 1/2-inch pieces

3 cups cooked rice

1/2 cup heavy cream

1 container lump crab meat,
 shells removed

Fry the bacon in a large saucepan over medium heat until cooked through. Chop the bacon and set aside. Reserve a small amount of the bacon drippings for the roux. Sauté the onion and garlic in the remaining bacon drippings for 5 minutes. Add the okra. Sauté for 10 minutes or until the okra is cooked through.

Heat the reserved bacon drippings in a large saucepan. Stir in a small amount of flour gradually. Cook until the roux is a smooth paste and light brown in color. Add the beef broth and a small amount of ham broth, stirring constantly. Cook until blended and thickened, stirring constantly. Add the vegetable juice cocktail, tomatoes, okra mixture, parsley, bacon, Tabasco sauce, Worcestershire sauce, saffron, salt, garlic salt and pepper in the order listed. Simmer for 10 minutes over medium-low heat, stirring frequently to keep from sticking to the bottom. You may cover while simmering.

Reduce the heat to the lowest setting. Add the shrimp and grouper and mix well. Add big spoonfuls of the rice at a time, mixing well after each addition. The shrimp and grouper should be cooked as soon as you finish adding the rice. Do not allow them to overcook. Remove from the heat. Add the cream and crab meat and mix well. Ladle into soup bowls.

ANNA CAM FENTRISS

Fiesta Chili

1/4 cup (1/2 stick) butter
1 small onion, minced
1 pound ground beef
1 envelope taco seasoning mix
1 envelope ranch salad
    dressing mix
1 cup water
1 (15-ounce) can whole kernel
    corn, drained and rinsed
1 (16-ounce) can pinto beans,
    drained and rinsed
1 (15-ounce) can black beans,
    drained and rinsed
1 (16-ounce) can kidney beans,
    drained and rinsed
1 cup water
1 (14-ounce) can Mexican-style
    diced tomatoes
1 (4-ounce) can green chiles
Small dash of cayenne pepper
1 cup sour cream

Melt the butter in a large saucepan over medium heat. Add the onion. Cook for 5 minutes or until the onion is translucent, stirring occasionally. Brown the ground beef in a skillet over medium heat, stirring until crumbly; drain. Add the taco seasoning mix, salad dressing mix and 1 cup water. Cook over medium heat for 3 to 4 minutes or until most of the liquid is absorbed, stirring occasionally. Remove from the heat. Stir the corn, beans and ground beef mixture into the onion. Add 1 cup water, the tomatoes, green chiles and cayenne pepper. Simmer, covered, for 30 minutes, stirring occasionally. Ladle into soup bowls and top with a dollop of sour cream. Serve with corn bread.

AMANDA CLEMENTS

LIGHTEN UP

Beans are loaded with protein, fiber, iron, vitamins, and other minerals and phytonutrients. Lower the sodium by rinsing the beans before adding them to any recipe. Look for the reduced-sodium taco seasoning mix and sodium-free corn and tomatoes. These changes will still make for a great-tasting bowl of chili.

Vegetable Beef Soup

1 to 2 pounds lean beef chuck or
  round, cubed
2 tablespoons vegetable oil
2 cups minced onion
2 cups sliced carrots
2 cups sliced celery
2 garlic cloves, minced
1 teaspoon salt
1 teaspoon pepper
1 (29-ounce) can diced tomatoes,
  or 2 (15-ounce) cans
3 cups vegetable stock or beef stock
1 bay leaf
4 whole allspice
1/2 cup minced parsley
2 cups chopped rutabaga (1 small)
Salt to taste

Brown the beef cubes in the oil in a large stockpot over
medium-high heat, turning frequently. Add the onion, carrots,
celery, garlic, 1 teaspoon salt and the pepper. Cook until the
onion is translucent. Add the tomatoes, vegetable stock, bay
leaf and allspice. Bring to a boil and reduce the heat. Simmer,
covered, for 2 hours. Add the parsley and rutabaga and mix
well. Simmer, covered, for 30 to 45 minutes or until the
rutabaga is tender. Adjust the salt to taste. Discard the bay
leaf. Ladle into soup bowls and serve with French bread. This
can be made a day or two in advance and reheated prior to
serving. Four vegetable or beef bouillon cubes dissolved in
3 cups water can be used instead of the stock.

TINA COUCH

Pasta and Sausage Soup

2 pounds hot or mild Italian
  sausage, casings removed
3 carrots, sliced
1 onion, chopped
4 garlic cloves, chopped
6 cups fat-skimmed chicken broth
2 (14-ounce) cans diced tomatoes
2 (15-ounce) cans cannellini,
  drained and rinsed
1 tablespoon dried basil
2 cups medium pasta shells
12 ounces spinach leaves, rinsed
Salt and pepper to taste
1 cup (4 ounces) grated
  Parmesan cheese

Cook the sausage in an 8- to 10-quart saucepan over high
heat for 8 to 10 minutes or until brown, stirring until crumbly.
Drain the sausage, reserving 1 tablespoon of the drippings in
the saucepan. Add the carrots, onion and garlic. Cook for 5 to
7 minutes or until the onion is tender, stirring frequently. Add
the sausage, broth, undrained tomatoes, beans and basil. Bring
to a boil. Add the pasta and reduce the heat. Simmer, covered,
for 10 minutes or until the pasta is tender, stirring occasionally.
Skim the surface and discard. Stir in the spinach. Cook for
30 seconds or until the spinach wilts. Add salt and pepper.
Ladle into soup bowls and sprinkle with the cheese.

ANN AND ELVIS BOGGAN

Golden Cheese Soup

SERVES 6 TO 8

2 tablespoons unsalted butter
1 onion, chopped
1/2 cup shredded carrots
1 cup very small broccoli florets
1 (15-ounce) can
   whole kernel corn
1/4 cup water
2 cups milk
2 (10-ounce) cans cream of
   potato soup
2 cups (8 ounces) shredded
   Cheddar cheese
Salt and pepper to taste
Fresh croissants

Melt the butter in a stockpot over medium heat. Add the onion and sauté until translucent. Add the carrots, broccoli, corn and water. Simmer, covered, for 5 to 10 minutes. Add the milk and soup. Bring to a boil. Reduce the heat to low. Stir in the cheese gradually. Add salt and pepper. Ladle into soup bowls and serve with warm croissants.

For a smooth bisque, purée the mixture in a food processor after bringing to a boil and before adding the cheese. Return to the saucepan and continue with the recipe.

AMANDA KARIOTH THOMPSON

White Bean Kielbasa Soup

SERVES 6 TO 8

2 cups finely chopped onions
2 cups sliced carrots
3 tablespoons chopped parsley
3 garlic cloves, chopped
1 teaspoon thyme
1 bay leaf
8 cups chicken broth
2 (15-ounce) cans Great
   Northern beans
1 red bell pepper, chopped
1 green bell pepper, chopped
2 cups chopped collard greens
1 pound kielbasa, sliced
1/4 cup (1/2 stick) butter

Combine the onions, carrots, parsley, garlic, thyme, bay leaf, broth, beans, bell peppers, collard greens, kielbasa and butter in a large saucepan and mix well. Cook over low heat for 1 hour. Discard the bay leaf. Ladle into soup bowls. Serve warm.

ORIGINALLY PUBLISHED IN *Finding Thyme*

LIGHTEN UP

Full of beans and greens, this nutritious soup is a hearty, healthy addition to any menu. Use low-fat kielbasa instead of the full-fat version, and substitute low-sodium chicken broth for the regular broth. Make these simple changes and, nutritionally speaking, you will have nearly the perfect cup of soup.

SOUPS & SALADS

{47}

French Lentil Soup

2 cups French lentils
6 cups water or vegetable broth
2 bay leaves
2 tablespoons olive oil
2 garlic cloves
1 onion, chopped
3 ribs celery, chopped
2 carrots, chopped
1 1/2 teaspoons sea salt
1 teaspoon dried tarragon
10 ounces baby spinach
1/2 cup tomato paste
Freshly ground pepper to taste
1/4 cup fresh parsley, finely
  chopped for garnish

Rinse and drain the lentils. Place the lentils, water and bay leaves in a large saucepan. Bring to a boil and reduce the heat. Simmer, covered, for 30 minutes or until the lentils are soft. Heat the olive oil in a skillet. Add the garlic and onion. Sauté until the onion is translucent. Add the celery, carrots, sea salt and tarragon. Cook until the vegetables are soft. Add to the cooked lentils. Add the baby spinach, tomato paste and additional water if needed. Cook, uncovered, for 15 minutes. Add pepper. Discard the bay leaves. Ladle into soup bowls. Garnish with the parsley.

EZZIE GOLDMAN

Simple Cream of Mushroom Soup

MAKES 4 CUPS

4 ounces sliced white mushrooms
6 tablespoons butter
5 tablespoons all-purpose flour
3 cups chicken broth
1 cup half-and-half
1/2 cup heavy whipping cream
Salt and pepper to taste
Fresh thyme leaves (optional)

Finely chop the mushrooms in a food processor. Melt the butter in a medium saucepan over medium-high heat. Add the mushrooms and sauté for 5 to 10 minutes or until soft. Whisk in the flour gradually. Add the broth gradually, whisking constantly. Reduce the heat to low. Cook for 10 minutes, stirring occasionally. Stir in the half-and-half, cream, salt and pepper. Ladle into soup bowls. Sprinkle with thyme leaves.

Potato Kale Soup

2 tablespoons butter
1 1/2 cups finely chopped onions
1 garlic clove, minced
7 cups chicken broth
4 cups coarsely chopped peeled
   Yukon Gold potatoes
1/2 teaspoon salt
1 bay leaf
6 cups fresh kale
1 teaspoon dried basil
2 ounces Gruyère cheese,
   shredded

Melt the butter in a large saucepan over medium heat. Add the onions. Cook for 8 minutes or until tender, stirring frequently. Add the garlic. Cook for 30 seconds, stirring constantly. Stir in the broth, potatoes, salt and bay leaf. Bring to a boil and reduce the heat. Simmer, covered, for 15 minutes. Stir in the kale and basil. Simmer, partially covered, for 30 minutes. Remove the bay leaf. Mash the potatoes partially with a potato masher until thick and chunky. Ladle into soup bowls. Top with the cheese.

JOYCE STILLWELL

Velvet Potato Soup

4 cups chopped potatoes
1 rib celery, minced
1 onion, minced
4 cups chicken broth
1/2 cup (1 stick) butter
2 cups milk
Salt to taste
1/4 teaspoon white pepper or
   black pepper
2/3 cup sour cream
1 cup heavy cream
1/4 cup all-purpose flour
Shredded Monterey Jack cheese
   with jalapeño chiles for garnish
Crumbled bacon for garnish
Chopped fresh chives for garnish

Place the potatoes, celery and onion in a large saucepan. Add the broth. Add enough water to fully cover the mixture if the broth does not. Cook for 30 minutes or until the potatoes are partially cooked through. Add the butter and milk. Bring to a slow boil, stirring frequently. Add salt and white pepper.

Mix the sour cream and heavy cream in a small bowl until blended. Stir in the flour gradually. Whisk into the potato mixture gradually. Cook until the potatoes are tender. Remove from the heat. Process with an immersion blender or in a food processor until smooth. Ladle into soup bowls. Garnish with the cheese, bacon and chives.

MARGARET HOLGATE

LIGHTEN UP

Cut back on the fat in this timeless classic by substituting reduced-fat 2% milk for the milk and cream. In addition to using lower-fat sour cream, reduce the butter and choose reduced-fat cheese. Hold down the sodium by using lower-sodium chicken broth and limiting any additions. This all adds up to a hearty and heart-healthy dish.

SOUPS & SALADS

Tarragon Butternut Squash Soup

1 large butternut squash
1¹/₂ cups chopped onions
1 tablespoon olive oil
2 garlic cloves
10¹/₂ cups chicken stock or broth
1 tablespoon brown sugar
1¹/₂ teaspoons chopped
 French tarragon
2 teaspoons chopped thyme
1 teaspoon pepper, or to taste
¹/₄ cup sour cream for garnish
¹/₄ cup chopped cooked bacon
 for garnish

Preheat the oven to 425 degrees. Cut the squash into halves lengthwise and remove the seeds. Spray the inside of the squash with nonstick cooking spray and place in a baking dish. Bake for 1 hour or until fork tender. Remove from the oven to cool. Remove the squash from the shell by cutting the flesh into a grid with a knife and flipping out of the shell.

Sauté the onions in the olive oil in a large saucepan until translucent. Add the garlic. Cook for 1 minute. Add the stock and bring to a boil. Reduce the heat to medium. Add the squash, brown sugar, tarragon, thyme and pepper. Cook, covered, for 15 minutes, stirring frequently. Remove from the heat. Purée in small batches in a food processor or blender. Return the soup to the saucepan. Cook over low heat until heated through. Ladle into soup bowls. Garnish with the sour cream and bacon.

AUDRA PEOPLES

Zucchini Jacked Soup

6 tablespoons butter, melted
6 zucchini, coarsely chopped
 (about 3 pounds)
2 Vidalia onions or other sweet
 onions, coarsely chopped
1 teaspoon salt
Freshly ground pepper to taste
2 cups chicken broth
1 cup milk
1 cup heavy cream
8 ounces Pepper Jack cheese
4 to 6 dashes of Tabasco sauce

Melt the butter in a large saucepan over medium-low heat. Add the zucchini, onions, salt and pepper. Cook, partially covered, for 45 minutes or until tender, stirring occasionally. Remove from the heat. Add the broth. Purée with an immersion blender or in a food processor fitted with a steel blade. Return to the saucepan. Stir in the milk and cream. Shred the cheese into the soup. Cook over medium-low heat until the cheese melts. Do not boil. Stir in the Tabasco sauce. Ladle into soup bowls.

Spinach Bacon Salad

DIJON MUSTARD
VINAIGRETTE
3 tablespoons red wine vinegar
1 teaspoon sugar
1/2 teaspoon Dijon mustard
1/4 cup extra-virgin olive oil

SALAD
5 slices bacon
1/3 cup sliced almonds
6 ounces fresh baby spinach
1 Granny Smith apple, chopped
3 to 4 scallions, chopped

To prepare the vinaigrette, whisk the vinegar, sugar and Dijon mustard in a bowl. Whisk in the olive oil gradually until blended.

To prepare the salad, fry the bacon in a skillet until crisp. Remove the bacon to paper towels to drain and cool. Crumble into bite-size pieces. Drain the skillet, reserving 1 tablespoon of the drippings in the skillet. Toast the almonds in the reserved drippings until light golden brown. Remove the almonds to paper towels to drain. Combine the spinach, apple and scallions in a large bowl. Add the almonds and bacon. Add the vinaigrette and toss to coat.

For variation, add 2 1/2 ounces blue cheese crumbles or substitute Almond Accents for the almonds.

Strawberry Spinach Salad

SESAME POPPY SEED
VINAIGRETTE
1/2 cup sugar
1/2 cup olive oil
1/4 cup distilled white vinegar
2 tablespoons sesame seeds
1 tablespoon poppy seeds
1 tablespoon minced onion
1/4 teaspoon paprika
1/4 teaspoon Worcestershire sauce

SALAD
10 ounces fresh spinach or baby
   salad greens, rinsed and drained
1 quart strawberries, sliced
1/4 cup almonds, blanched
   and slivered

To prepare the vinaigrette, whisk the sugar, olive oil, vinegar, sesame seeds, poppy seeds, onion, paprika and Worcestershire sauce in a bowl until mixed.

To prepare the salad, combine the spinach, strawberries and almonds in a large bowl. Add the vinaigrette and toss to coat. Chill for 10 to 15 minutes before serving.

STACEY SPEER

Cherries Vinaigrette and Goat Cheese Salad

SERVES 4 TO 6

CHERRIES VINAIGRETTE
1 1/4 cups dried cherries
1/2 cup port
5 ounces thick bacon, chopped
2 shallots, minced
1 garlic clove, minced
1/3 cup olive oil
1/4 cup white wine vinegar
2 teaspoons sugar
Salt and pepper to taste

SALAD
8 ounces mixed baby greens
1/2 cup pine nuts, toasted
4 ounces goat cheese, crumbled

To prepare the vinaigrette, simmer the cherries and port in a saucepan for 2 minutes. Remove from the heat to cool. Fry the bacon in a skillet until crisp. Drain the bacon, leaving 1 tablespoon of the drippings in the skillet. Add the shallots and garlic. Cook for 2 minutes. Add the olive oil, vinegar and sugar. Cook until the sugar dissolves, stirring constantly. Stir in the cherry mixture. Add salt and pepper. Keep warm.

To prepare the salad, combine the baby greens and pine nuts in a large bowl. When ready to serve, pour the warm vinaigrette over the baby greens. Sprinkle with the goat cheese.

ORIGINALLY PUBLISHED IN *Finding Thyme*

Photograph for this recipe appears on page 38.

Blue Cranberry Salad

SERVES 8 TO 10

10 ounces salad greens
3 to 4 radishes, chopped
3 to 4 scallions, chopped
1/2 cup dried cranberries
1/2 cup walnuts
1/2 cup chopped celery
1 cup chopped broccoli (optional)
Fresh dill weed to taste
Blue cheese salad dressing
Balsamic vinaigrette

Combine the salad greens, radishes, scallions, cranberries, walnuts, celery, broccoli and dill weed in a large bowl. Mix equal parts of blue cheese salad dressing and balsamic vinaigrette in a bowl. Pour over the salad and toss to evenly coat.

AMANDA CLEMENTS

TALLAHASSEE TIDBIT
The Junior League of Tallahassee was one of the founding organizations for the Tallahassee Museum. The popular Discovery Center and the playground at the Tallahassee Museum were made possible due to the Junior League of Tallahassee's leadership and support.

Chopped Salad

BALSAMIC VINAIGRETTE
1/4 cup balsamic vinegar
1 teaspoon sugar
1/2 teaspoon salt
Freshly ground pepper to taste
1 teaspoon Dijon mustard
1/2 cup olive oil

SALAD
1 head romaine
1 small head radicchio
2 small Kirby, Chinese or
   English cucumbers, peeled
   and chopped
1/4 purple onion, chopped
2 radishes, chopped
1/2 red bell pepper, chopped
10 grape tomatoes,
   cut into quarters
2 slices bacon, crisp-cooked
   and crumbled
1/4 cup dried cranberries
4 ounces Gorgonzola
   cheese, crumbled

To prepare the vinaigrette, combine the vinegar, sugar, salt and pepper in a bowl or shaker and whisk or shake to mix. Add the Dijon mustard and mix well. Add the olive oil and mix vigorously.

To prepare the salad, cut the romaine and radicchio lengthwise, holding them intact. Cut crosswise to form small chopped leaves and place in a large salad bowl. Add the cucumbers, onion, radishes, bell pepper, tomatoes, bacon, cranberries and cheese. Add the vinaigrette to taste and toss to coat. Store the remaining vinaigrette in the refrigerator. For variation, add chopped cooked chicken.

RISE VILLANUEVA

LIGHTEN UP

Salads can be a high-fiber, high-nutrient addition to any diet, but beware of how they are dressed. To cut the fat in this recipe, reduce the 1/2 cup olive oil that provides a whopping 64 grams of fat and 960 calories. Replace a portion of the olive oil with fruit juice or water for a lighter vinaigrette.

Italian Dinner Salad

SERVES 6

1 package spring salad mix

1/2 cucumber, peeled and sliced

1/2 Cubanelle pepper, sliced

1/2 red onion, thinly sliced
  into rings

12 black olives

15 grape tomatoes, cut into halves

3 to 4 fresh basil leaves, minced

1/4 teaspoon dill weed

3 to 4 ounces feta
  cheese, crumbled

1 envelope Italian salad
  dressing mix

Combine the salad mix, cucumber, Cubanelle pepper, onion, olives and tomatoes in a salad bowl. Add the basil and dill weed and toss to mix. Sprinkle with the feta cheese. Prepare the salad dressing mix using the package directions. Pour the salad dressing to taste over the salad and toss to coat.

Confetti Coleslaw

SERVES 10 TO 12

COLESLAW DRESSING

1/2 cup mayonnaise

1 tablespoon sweet pickle relish

1 tablespoon honey mustard

1 tablespoon honey

Salt and pepper to taste

COLESLAW

5 cups cabbage, shredded

1/2 cup slivered almonds, toasted

1 1/2 cups dried cranberries

1/2 cup chopped celery

1/4 cup sliced scallions

1/2 cup chopped green
  bell pepper

To prepare the dressing, combine the mayonnaise, sweet pickle relish, honey mustard and honey in a dressing shaker and shake well. Add salt and pepper. Chill until serving time.

To prepare the coleslaw, combine the cabbage, almonds, cranberries, celery, scallions and bell pepper in a large bowl or large sealable plastic bag and toss to mix. Store, covered, in the refrigerator until serving time. To serve, pour the dressing over the cabbage mixture and toss to coat.

BARBARA CORVEN

LIGHTEN UP

This recipe is full of nutritional crunch. Cabbage is a cruciferous vegetable with nutrients that make it a real cancer fighter. Dried cranberries also fit the nutrition bill by providing several different antioxidants. By toasting the almonds, you get a flavor boost so you can use less without sacrificing flavor. Lighten the recipe further by substituting reduced-fat mayonnaise in place of regular.

Nutty Broccoli Slaw

SERVES 16

1 (3-ounce) package chicken-
   flavored ramen noodles
1 (12-ounce) package
   broccoli slaw
1 (12-ounce) package fresh
   broccoli florets, cut into
   small pieces
2 cups sliced scallions
1 cup chopped red bell pepper
1 cup sunflower seeds, toasted
1/2 cup slivered almonds, toasted
1 cup dried cranberries
1/2 cup sugar
1/2 cup olive oil
1/2 cup cider vinegar

Break the ramen noodles into small pieces while still in the package. Reserve the flavor packet for the dressing. Combine the broccoli slaw, broccoli pieces, scallions, bell pepper, sunflower seeds, almonds, cranberries and the ramen noodle pieces and toss to mix. Chill, covered, until serving time.

Combine the sugar, olive oil, vinegar and the contents of the reserved flavoring packet in a bowl and mix well. Chill, covered, until serving time. To serve, pour the dressing over the broccoli mixture and toss to coat.

JILLIAN HOOVER

Sweet Potato Salad

SERVES 6 TO 8

2 1/2 pounds sweet potatoes
1 tablespoon Dijon mustard
4 teaspoons white wine vinegar
1/2 teaspoon salt
Dash of garlic powder
1/4 cup olive oil
4 scallions, sliced
1/2 red bell pepper, chopped
1/2 cup crumbled bacon

Peel the sweet potatoes and cut into 1-inch pieces. Steam the sweet potatoes, covered, for 10 to 12 minutes or until tender. Place in a bowl and set aside. Whisk the Dijon mustard, vinegar, salt and garlic powder in a bowl. Add the olive oil gradually, whisking until emulsified. Pour over the warm sweet potatoes. Let cool to room temperature. Add the scallions, bell pepper and bacon just before serving and toss to mix. You may prepare up to 2 hours before serving.

MARTHA GENE WIGGINTON

Florida Sunshine Salad

GINGER CITRUS DRESSING

1/4 cup fresh pink grapefruit juice
2 tablespoons fresh lime juice
1 tablespoon honey
1 tablespoon grated fresh ginger
1 small shallot, minced
1/2 cup olive oil
Splash of sesame oil
Sea salt and freshly ground
  pepper to taste

SALAD

2 lobster tails, split lengthwise
  leaving meat in shell, or 16 to
  20 large Florida shrimp
1 tablespoon vegetable oil
Sea salt and pepper to taste
8 ounces fresh spinach,
  stems removed
8 ounces garden fresh
  mixed greens
2 large Florida red
  grapefruit, sectioned
1 small avocado, cut into
  bite-size pieces
1 mango, cut into bite-size pieces
1/2 cup pecans, toasted
1/2 cup crumbled fresh chèvre

To prepare the dressing, whisk the grapefruit juice, lime juice, honey, ginger and shallot in a small bowl. Whisk in the olive oil and sesame oil gradually. Add sea salt and pepper.

To prepare the salad, preheat a charcoal grill. Drizzle the lobster tails with vegetable oil to prevent sticking. Sprinkle with sea salt and pepper. Place meat side down on a grill rack. Grill for 2 to 3 minutes. Turn and grill for a few minutes or until the lobster meat is opaque. Do not overcook. Remove to a platter to cool. Place the spinach and mixed greens in a large bowl. Toss with enough dressing to coat. Divide the greens among four salad plates. Top with the grapefruit, avocado, mango, pecans and cheese. Remove the lobster meat from the shell and divide evenly on top of each salad. Drizzle some of the remaining dressing over the lobster meat and serve.

CHEF JOSH BUTLER, FLORIDA GOVERNOR'S MANSION

TALLAHASSEE TIDBIT
Wakulla Springs, south of Tallahassee, is the largest (4 acres) and deepest (185 feet) freshwater springs in the world, disgorging 400,000 to 600,000 gallons of water per minute. The springs have been the setting for numerous movies, such as several Tarzan movies starring Johnny Weismuller and Maureen O'Sullivan, as well as Creature from the Black Lagoon *and* Airport '77.

Mediterranean Pasta Salad

SERVES 8 TO 10

2 (15-ounce) cans chick-peas
2 (14-ounce) cans artichoke hearts
1 pound tomatoes, chopped
 (about 3 cups)
1 small red onion, finely chopped
1/2 cup pine nuts, toasted
1/4 cup finely chopped black olives
2 tablespoons capers
12 ounces crumbled feta cheese
1/4 cup red wine vinegar
Zest of 1 lemon
Juice of 2 lemons
1/4 teaspoon salt
1/4 teaspoon freshly ground
 black pepper
1 (8-ounce) bottle Greek
 salad dressing
16 ounces corkscrew pasta,
 such as rotini, farfalle or fusilli

Drain the chick-peas and artichoke hearts and rinse. Remove the small leaves from the artichoke hearts until only the heart is left. Place the artichoke hearts in a large bowl. Mince the chick-peas and add to the artichoke hearts. Add the tomatoes, onion, pine nuts, olives, capers, feta cheese, vinegar, lemon zest, lemon juice, salt, pepper and salad dressing and mix well. Marinate in the refrigerator for 1 hour or longer.

Cook the pasta in boiling water in a large stockpot just until tender; drain. Add to the artichoke mixture and toss well. Chill, covered, in the refrigerator until serving time.

Asian Chicken Salad

SERVES 6 TO 8

3/4 cup soy sauce
1/4 cup sherry
1/4 cup peanut oil
2 tablespoons sesame oil
2 tablespoons honey
3 tablespoons brown sugar
3 cups chopped cooked chicken
8 ounces linguini
1 (9-ounce) package frozen
 snow peas
1/2 head (about 3 stalks)
 bok choy, chopped
1 (8-ounce) can water chestnuts,
 drained and sliced
4 scallions, sliced
3/4 cup chopped cashews

Combine the soy sauce, sherry, peanut oil, sesame oil, honey and brown sugar in a food processor and process until blended. Pour one-half of the dressing over the chicken into a bowl. Chill, covered, for 2 hours or longer. Break the pasta into halves and cook using the package directions; drain. Rinse with cold water; drain and place in a large bowl. Cook the snow peas using the package directions; drain. Rinse with cold water; drain. Add the snow peas, bok choy, water chestnuts, scallions and remaining dressing to the pasta and stir gently. Add the chicken and stir gently. Chill, covered, until ready to serve. Stir in the cashews just before serving.

LINZY FOSTER

Chicken Salad Supreme

SERVES 10

10 chicken breast halves, boned
  and skinned
1 teaspoon crushed rosemary
1 teaspoon thyme
1 teaspoon salt
1/4 teaspoon freshly ground pepper
2 envelopes dry Italian salad
  dressing mix
1 cup crumbled cooked bacon
  (about 8 to 12 ounces)
1/4 cup slivered almonds
1 1/3 cups green grapes,
  cut into halves
3 tablespoons mayonnaise
2 teaspoons mustard
Lettuce leaves or cantaloupe slices

Fill a large skillet half full of water. Place the chicken, rosemary, thyme, salt and pepper in the water. Cook over medium heat until the chicken is cooked through. Prepare the salad dressing mix using the package directions. Pour into a 3-quart shallow dish. Place the hot chicken in the salad dressing. Marinate, covered, in the refrigerator for 3 hours. Drain the chicken, reserving 2 tablespoons of the marinade. Cut the chicken into cubes and place in a bowl. Add the reserved marinade and toss well. Add the bacon, almonds and grapes and mix well. Mix the mayonnaise and mustard in a bowl. Add to the chicken mixture one tablespoon at a time, mixing until the salad holds together. Spoon into the lettuce leaves to serve.

ORIGINALLY PUBLISHED IN *Thymes Remembered*

Curried Chicken Salad

SERVES 4

2 cups cubed rotisserie chicken
1/2 Vidalia onion or other sweet
  onion, chopped
1 rib celery, chopped
1/4 cup pecans, toasted and
  coarsely chopped
1/3 cup assorted dried fruit, such
  as golden raisins, cranberries,
  blueberries, cherries or
  chopped apricots
1/2 cup mayonnaise
2 teaspoons mild curry powder
4 large romaine cups

Combine the chicken, onion and celery in a bowl. Add the pecans and dried fruit and toss to mix. Mix the mayonnaise and curry powder in a small bowl. Fold into the chicken mixture, trying not to break up the chicken. Chill, covered, in the refrigerator. Spoon into the romaine cups to serve.

RISE VILLANUEVA

LIGHTEN UP
Dried fruits added to this chicken salad not only add a touch of taste, but also fiber, vitamins, and minerals. Dried fruit is a portable snack and a great addition to salads, bread recipes, or even a bowl of cereal. Cherries, cranberries, and apricots are especially rich in phytochemicals, which are plant compounds that aid in the prevention of heart disease and several forms of cancer.

Cobb Salad with Herbed Buttermilk Dressing

SERVES 4

HERBED BUTTERMILK DRESSING

2/3 cup well-shaken buttermilk

1/3 cup Greek-style plain yogurt

Juice of 1 lemon

2 tablespoons finely chopped fresh basil

2 tablespoons finely chopped Mexican tarragon or regular tarragon

1 tablespoon finely chopped oregano

1 small garlic clove, minced

1/4 teaspoon (heaping) salt

Pepper to taste

SALAD

1 head Florida romaine, rinsed and finely chopped

1 head Florida butter crunch or Bibb lettuce, rinsed and finely chopped

2 boneless skinless chicken breasts, grilled and cut into cubes

6 slices applewood smoked bacon, crisp-cooked and finely chopped

1 pint Florida grape tomatoes

3 ripe Florida avocados, cut into 1/2-inch pieces

2 tablespoons chopped fresh chives

1 hard-cooked egg, chopped

1/2 cup crumbled blue cheese

To prepare the dressing, whisk the buttermilk, yogurt, lemon juice, basil, tarragon, oregano and garlic in a small bowl. Add the salt and pepper. Chill, covered, for 1 hour or longer to allow the flavors to meld.

To prepare the salad, toss the lettuce together in a large bowl. Arrange the grilled chicken, bacon, tomatoes and avocados decoratively over the greens. Drizzle with some of the dressing. Sprinkle with the chives, egg and blue cheese.

This is Florida Governor Crist's favorite salad.

CHEF JOSH BUTLER, FLORIDA GOVERNOR'S MANSION

TALLAHASSEE TIDBIT

America's largest concentration of original plantations—300,000 acres, 71 plantations—exists in the 30-mile span between Tallahassee and Thomasville, Georgia.

Sides

[sahyd•s]

Tasty accompaniment to an entrée;

delicious enough to serve alone.

Asparagus Risotto

1 pound fresh asparagus, cut into
  bite-size pieces
4 cups chicken broth
1/4 cup (1/2 stick) butter
1/2 cup chopped Vidalia onion or
  other sweet onion
2 garlic cloves, minced
1 cup arborio rice
1 cup dry white wine
1 teaspoon chopped fresh thyme
1/2 teaspoon pepper
1 cup (4 ounces) grated
  Parmesan cheese

Bring the asparagus and 1/4 cup of the broth to a boil in a Dutch oven over medium-high heat. Cook for 10 minutes or until tender. Remove the asparagus with a slotted spoon and set aside. Bring the remaining 3 3/4 cups broth to a simmer in a saucepan. Do not boil. Keep warm over low heat.

Stir the butter, onion and garlic into the remaining broth in the Dutch oven. Cook for 3 minutes. Add the rice and wine. Cook for 5 minutes or until the liquid is absorbed, stirring constantly. Reduce the heat to medium. Add 1 cup of the simmering broth. Cook until the liquid is absorbed, stirring frequently.

Repeat the procedure with the remaining simmering broth 1 cup at a time until all the broth is used, checking frequently because you do not want the risotto too firm or too soft. The total cooking time will be about 15 to 20 minutes. Remove from the heat. Stir in the asparagus, thyme, pepper and cheese. Serve immediately. You may substitute 1 pound steamed green beans for the asparagus, if desired.

AMANDA WHITAKER

Photograph for this recipe appears on page 60.

LIGHTEN UP

Asparagus, with its bright green stalks, is low in calories, high in fiber, and contains vitamin A, vitamin C, and folic acid. To keep asparagus fresh longer, trim a little bit off the ends and stand the spears cut end down in an inch of water. Make all fruits and vegetables a key component in your healthy eating plan.

A THYME TO CELEBRATE

Oven-Roasted Asparagus with Toasted Almonds

SERVES 4 TO 6

2 pounds fresh asparagus
2 tablespoons olive oil
2 garlic cloves, minced
1/2 teaspoon salt
1/2 teaspoon freshly ground pepper
1/2 cup sliced almonds, toasted

Preheat the oven to 350 degrees. Snap off and discard the tough ends of the asparagus. Place the asparagus on a lightly greased baking sheet. Drizzle with the olive oil. Sprinkle with the garlic, salt and pepper. Bake for 10 minutes or until the desired tenderness. Remove to a serving dish and sprinkle with the almonds.

AMANDA WHITAKER

Best Baked Beans

SERVES 7 TO 10

2 (16-ounce) cans baked beans
1 pound country sausage, sliced
1 onion, chopped
1/4 cup packed brown sugar
1/4 cup ketchup
1 tablespoon mustard
1/4 cup strong coffee
1/4 cup maple syrup

Preheat the oven to 300 degrees. Combine the beans, sausage, onion, brown sugar, ketchup, mustard, coffee and maple syrup in a bowl and mix well. Spoon into a deep baking dish. Bake, covered, for 1 hour. Uncover and bake for 30 to 45 minutes longer or until the desired consistency.

BETTYE "BEBE" ATKINSON

Lemon Broccoli

SERVES 6

1 head fresh broccoli,
  cut into florets
2/3 cup sour cream
1/3 cup mayonnaise
Juice of 1 lemon
Thinly sliced lemon for garnish

Steam the broccoli until tender-crisp and drain. Place in a serving dish. Combine the sour cream, mayonnaise and lemon juice in a small saucepan. Cook over medium heat until smooth and creamy. Drizzle over the broccoli and toss lightly. Garnish with thinly sliced lemon.

SHARON COLLEY

Broccoli and Spinach Casserole

SERVES 4 TO 6

1 (10-ounce) package frozen chopped broccoli, thawed and drained

1 (10-ounce) package frozen chopped spinach, thawed and drained

1/3 cup chopped onion

2 tablespoons extra-virgin olive oil

1 cup sour cream

2 tablespoons mayonnaise

1 egg, well beaten

1 (10-ounce) can cream of mushroom soup, or 3/4 cup Simple Cream of Mushroom Soup (page 48)

3/4 cup bread crumbs

1/4 teaspoon pepper

1 1/2 cups (6 ounces) shredded sharp Cheddar cheese

Salt to taste

Preheat the oven to 350 degrees. Mix the broccoli and spinach in a large bowl. Sauté the onion in the olive oil in a skillet until translucent. Add to the broccoli mixture and mix well.

Combine the sour cream, mayonnaise, egg, soup, bread crumbs and pepper in a large bowl and mix well. Fold in the broccoli mixture. Add 1 cup of the cheese and mix well. Add the salt. Spoon into a lightly buttered 2-quart baking dish. Sprinkle the remaining 1/2 cup cheese over the top. Bake, uncovered, for 30 to 45 minutes or until the cheese is bubbly. Remove from the oven and let stand for 10 minutes before serving.

Brussels Sprout Sauté

SERVES 4 TO 6

1 pound brussels sprouts

3 tablespoons extra-virgin olive oil

1 Vidalia onion or other sweet onion, finely sliced

Juice of 1 lemon

Salt and freshly ground pepper to taste

1/4 cup water

Trim the brussels sprouts of the outermost leaves and cut into halves lengthwise. Heat the olive oil in a large skillet over medium-high heat. Add the brussels sprouts. Sauté for 5 to 6 minutes or until light brown. Add the onion. Sauté for 5 to 6 minutes or until the onion is translucent. Add the lemon juice, salt, pepper and water. Cook, covered, for 5 to 6 minutes or until the brussels sprouts are tender.

Quick-and-Easy
Collard Green Potpie

2 (14-ounce) cans seasoned
   collard greens, or 8 cups fresh
1 large onion, chopped
1/4 cup olive oil or bacon drippings
1/2 cup all-purpose flour
1 (10-ounce) can vegetable broth
1 tablespoon sugar
Salt and pepper to taste
Hot red pepper sauce to taste
2 (9-ounce) packages corn
   muffin mix
Crumbled bacon for garnish
Shredded Cheddar cheese
   for garnish
Chopped scallions for garnish

Preheat the oven to 375 degrees. Drain the collard greens, reserving the liquid. Sauté the onion in the olive oil in a skillet until tender. Stir in the flour. Add the reserved liquid. Cook until smooth and creamy, adding some of the vegetable broth if the mixture is too thick. Add the collard greens, sugar, salt, pepper and hot sauce and mix well.

Spread evenly into a 9×12-inch baking dish. Prepare the muffin mix using the package directions. Spread the batter over the collard green mixture. Bake for 20 minutes or until the topping is brown around the edges. Garnish with crumbled bacon, shredded Cheddar cheese and chopped scallions.

MELINDA MCDANIEL, THE MARINATED MUSHROOM

Lemon-Glazed Carrots

SERVES 4

1 pound carrots
Salt to taste
3 tablespoons butter
2 tablespoons sugar
4 thin slices lemon

Peel the carrots and cut into 1-inch pieces. Place in a medium saucepan with enough salted water to cover. Simmer, covered, for 15 minutes or until tender; drain.

Melt the butter in a heavy medium skillet. Stir in the sugar. Add the lemon slices and carrots. Cook over medium heat until the carrots are glazed, stirring occasionally.

NELLA SCHOMBURGER

Cauliflower Gratin

4 slices fresh bread
1/4 cup (1 ounce) grated
  Parmesan cheese
1/4 cup (1/2 stick) unsalted butter
1/4 cup all-purpose flour
3 cups whole or reduced-fat milk
1 teaspoon salt
1/2 teaspoon black pepper
1/4 teaspoon nutmeg
1/8 to 1/4 teaspoon cayenne pepper
1 head cauliflower, cut into florets
  (about 3 pounds)
1 cup (4 ounces) grated
  Parmesan cheese

Preheat the oven to 350 degrees. Pulse the bread and 1/4 cup cheese in a food processor or blender three to five times or until coarse crumbs form. Melt the butter in a large saucepan over medium heat. Whisk in the flour. Cook for 1 to 2 minutes, whisking constantly. Whisk in the milk. Add the salt, black pepper, nutmeg and cayenne pepper. Add the cauliflower. Bring to a boil and reduce the heat.

Simmer, covered, for 8 minutes. Turn off the heat. Stir in 1 cup cheese gradually. Pour into a 9×13-inch baking dish. Sprinkle with the bread crumb mixture. Bake, covered with foil, for 15 to 20 minutes or until the cauliflower is tender. Remove the foil. Bake for 15 minutes longer or until the bread crumbs are golden brown. Broil for 1 to 2 minutes or until brown and bubbly, checking frequently.

Potato Cauliflower Purée

1 1/4 pounds cauliflower with
  2-inch stems, broken into
  small pieces
1 boiling potato, peeled and cut
  into small pieces
1/2 cup whipping cream
1/2 cup (2 ounces) freshly grated
  Parmesan cheese
3 tablespoons butter
1/8 teaspoon white pepper
Large pinch of freshly
  grated nutmeg
Salt to taste

Steam the cauliflower with the potato for 12 minutes or until soft. Process the vegetables one-half at a time in a food processor until pureed. Combine with the cream, cheese, butter, white pepper and nutmeg in a bowl and mix until smooth. Add salt. Serve immediately.

NELLA SCHOMBURGER

Gruyère Thyme Potatoes

2 1/2 pounds Yukon Gold potatoes,
   peeled and sliced (about 3)
Salt to taste
1 1/2 cups (6 ounces) shredded
   Gruyère cheese
1 cup large shallots, chopped
1/2 cup (2 ounces) grated
   Parmesan cheese
1 teaspoon dried thyme
Pepper to taste
2 tablespoons unsalted
   butter, softened
2 cups heavy cream

Preheat the oven to 350 degrees. Boil the potatoes in salted water in a large saucepan for 25 minutes or until tender; drain. Combine the Gruyère cheese, shallots, Parmesan cheese, thyme, salt and pepper in a medium bowl and mix well. Grease a 4-quart baking dish with the butter.

Layer the potatoes and cheese mixture alternately in the prepared baking dish, ending with the cheese mixture. Pour the cream over the layers. Bake for 50 to 60 minutes or until the top is golden brown. Let stand for 10 minutes before serving.

This dish can be prepared ahead and stored in the refrigerator. Add 10 to 15 minutes to the baking time.

Vermont Cheddar Potatoes

1 (32-ounce) package frozen
   Southern-style hash brown
   potatoes, thawed
3 cups (12 ounces) shredded
   sharp white Vermont
   Cheddar cheese
2 tablespoons all-purpose flour
Salt and pepper to taste
2 cups half-and-half
Paprika to taste

Preheat the oven to 350 degrees. Combine the potatoes, cheese, flour, salt and pepper in a large sealable freezer bag. Seal the bag and shake vigorously for a few minutes. Place in a buttered 9×13-inch baking dish. Pour the half-and-half evenly over the mixture. Sprinkle lightly with paprika. Bake for 30 to 45 minutes or until bubbly and cooked through. For additional flavor, add 1 cup crumbled crisp-cooked bacon to the potato mixture before baking.

SHARON COLLEY

Sweet Potatoes with Maple Ginger Cream

SERVES 4

4 sweet potatoes
1/2 cup sour cream
2 tablespoons maple syrup
1/4 teaspoon salt
1/4 teaspoon ginger
1/4 cup chopped pecans, toasted

Preheat the oven to 375 degrees. Pierce the sweet potatoes with a fork and place on a baking sheet. Bake for 1 hour. Split the sweet potatoes. Combine the sour cream, maple syrup, salt and ginger in a bowl and mix well. Spoon into the sweet potatoes and sprinkle with the pecans.

ORIGINALLY PUBLISHED IN *Finding Thyme*

Spinach and Mushroom Pie

SERVES 6

1 (10-ounce) package frozen
   chopped spinach, thawed and
   drained
1/2 cup chopped onion
1/2 cup chopped mushrooms
2 tablespoons butter
1/4 teaspoon salt
1/4 teaspoon pepper
1/4 teaspoon nutmeg
3 eggs
1 cup cottage cheese
1/2 cup light cream
1/4 cup (1 ounce) grated
   Parmesan cheese
1 unbaked (9-inch) pie shell

Preheat the oven to 350 degrees. Thaw the spinach and drain well. Sauté the onion and mushrooms in the butter in a skillet until the onion is translucent. Remove from the heat. Stir in the spinach, salt, pepper and nutmeg. Beat the eggs lightly in a bowl. Add the cottage cheese, cream and Parmesan cheese and mix well. Stir in the spinach mixture. Pour into the pie shell. Bake for 50 minutes or until the center tests done. Let stand for 10 minutes before serving.

MARY JAYNE SOKOLOW

TALLAHASSEE TIDBIT
Althea Gibson, who graduated from Florida A&M University, was the first African-American to win a Grand Slam tennis championship when she won the 1957 women's singles title at Wimbledon.

Posh Squash

1 1/2 pounds yellow squash, sliced

1 1/2 pounds zucchini, sliced

1 onion, chopped

Salt to taste

2 eggs

3/4 cup mayonnaise

3/4 cup (3 ounces) grated
   Parmesan cheese

1/2 teaspoon pepper

3/4 cup panko (Japanese
   bread crumbs)

3 tablespoons butter, melted

Preheat the oven to 350 degrees. Simmer the squash, zucchini and onion in lightly salted water in a saucepan for 30 minutes or until tender. Drain well and let stand until cool.

Mix the egg, mayonnaise, cheese and pepper in a bowl. Fold in the squash mixture. Spoon into a buttered baking dish. Sprinkle with the panko. Drizzle with the butter. Bake for 30 minutes or until the topping is golden brown. Let stand for 10 minutes before serving.

SARA BETH SHIPPEN

Squash Casserole

2 1/2 to 3 pounds squash, sliced

1 Vidalia onion or other sweet
   onion, chopped

1/2 cup (1 stick) butter, melted

2 eggs

2 cups (8 ounces) sharp Cheddar
   cheese, shredded

1/2 sleeve saltine crackers,
   finely crushed

Salt and pepper to taste

Preheat the oven to 350 degrees. Boil the squash and onion in water in a saucepan until tender; drain. Mash the squash and onion. Add the butter, eggs, cheese, cracker crumbs, salt and pepper and mix well. Spoon into a baking dish. Bake for 30 to 45 minutes or until heated through.

PAM EDWARDS

Zucchini Tomato Gratin

SERVES 6 TO 8

3 eggs

1 1/2 cups Italian-seasoned panko
  (Japanese bread crumbs)

1 teaspoon salt

2 tablespoons extra-virgin olive oil

3 zucchini, cut into 1/3-inch-
  thick slices

5 Roma tomatoes, seeded
  and chopped

1 teaspoon salt

1/2 teaspoon pepper

2 teaspoons extra-virgin olive oil

1 cup sour cream

1 cup (4 ounces) grated good-
  quality Parmesan cheese

Preheat the oven to 350 degrees. Whisk the eggs in a bowl. Mix the panko with 1 teaspoon salt in a shallow dish. Heat 2 tablespoons olive oil in a large skillet over medium-high heat. Dip each zucchini slice in the eggs and then coat with the panko mixture. Fry in batches in the hot olive oil for 5 minutes per side or until golden brown. Combine the tomatoes, 1 teaspoon salt and the pepper in a bowl. Add 2 teaspoons olive oil and toss to coat.

Layer the zucchini, sour cream, tomato mixture and Parmesan cheese one-third at a time in a buttered square baking dish. Bake for 35 to 40 minutes or until cooked through.

Turn this side dish into a vegetarian entrée by adding 1 to 2 cups hot cooked pasta to the tomato mixture.

GINA COLLEY-HOLGATE

Roasted Tomatoes with Feta Cheese, Olives and Pine Nuts

SERVES 6

6 plum tomatoes, cut into halves
  lengthwise and seeded

Salt and pepper to taste

1/4 cup pine nuts

1 cup crumbled feta cheese

1 1/2 ounces cream cheese

1/3 cup kalamata olives, chopped

1 teaspoon dried oregano

1 tablespoon extra-virgin olive oil

Preheat the oven to 325 degrees. Sprinkle the tomatoes with salt and pepper. Place cut side down on a wire rack set over a baking sheet. Let drain for 30 minutes. Sauté the pine nuts in a skillet over low heat for 3 to 4 minutes or until golden brown. Mix the feta cheese, cream cheese, olives, pine nuts and oregano in a bowl. Fill each tomato with about 2 tablespoons of the feta mixture. Place in a baking pan. Bake for 30 minutes or until soft. Drizzle with the olive oil. Serve hot, warm or at room temperature.

AGGIE BELL

Tomato Basil Tart with Spinach

SERVES 8

1 (1-crust) pie pastry
1/2 cup (2 ounces) shredded
  mozzarella cheese
1 cup fresh basil, cut into strips
3 to 5 garlic cloves, pressed
1 cup (4 ounces) shredded
  mozzarella cheese
1/4 cup (1 ounce) grated
  Parmesan cheese
1/2 cup mayonnaise
Dash of pepper
1/2 package fresh spinach, rinsed
  and patted dry
4 tomatoes, or 5 Roma tomatoes,
  sliced and drained

Preheat the oven to 375 degrees. Fit the pastry into a 9-inch pie plate, fluting the edge. Bake until light brown. Sprinkle 1/2 cup mozzarella cheese into the hot piecrust and let stand until melted. Mix the basil and garlic in a bowl. Combine 1 cup mozzarella cheese, the Parmesan cheese, mayonnaise and pepper in a bowl and mix well.

Layer the spinach over the melted cheese. The layer will be thick but will shrink during baking. Arrange the tomatoes over the spinach. Cover with the basil mixture. Spread the mozzarella mixture evenly over the top. Sprinkle with additional shredded mozzarella cheese, if desired. Bake for 30 minutes or until the top is golden brown and bubbly. Remove from the oven and let stand for 5 to 10 minutes before serving.

SARA J. MARCHESSAULT

THYME SAVER

Place stem-on fresh herbs in a glass of water and store in the refrigerator. Change the water occasionally and the herbs will stay fresh and green much longer. Don't try this with basil, however; it hates to be cold. Keep basil in a water-filled glass on your kitchen counter at room temperature for maximum freshness.

SIDES

{71}

Tomato Sauce

2 tablespoons extra-virgin
  olive oil
1 large Vidalia onion or other
  sweet onion, finely chopped
3 garlic cloves, crushed
1 tablespoon Italian seasoning
2 (28-ounce) cans crushed
  tomatoes
1 to 2 teaspoons salt
1/2 teaspoon black pepper
1 teaspoon red pepper flakes
1 to 2 teaspoons sugar

Heat the olive oil in a large saucepan over medium to medium-high heat. Add the onion. Sauté for 10 minutes or until translucent. Add the garlic and Italian seasoning. Sauté for 2 minutes. Do not brown the garlic. Stir in the tomatoes and bring to a simmer. Stir in 1 teaspoon salt, the black pepper, red pepper flakes and 1 teaspoon sugar. Simmer for 45 minutes, stirring frequently to prevent sticking to the bottom of the pan. Adjust the seasonings to taste. For Tomato Basil Sauce, substitute 1 tablespoon chopped fresh basil for the Italian seasoning.

For Creamy Tomato Sauce, add 1/2 cup heavy whipping cream just before serving.

Pasta Alfresco

1 teaspoon extra-virgin olive oil
1 teaspoon chopped fresh basil
1 garlic clove, minced
1 teaspoon oregano
1 (14-ounce) can diced tomatoes
  with basil, garlic and oregano
1 (14-ounce) can chicken broth,
  plus additional if needed
9 ounces fresh linguini
1/4 cup (1 ounce) freshly grated
  Parmesan cheese
Fresh basil for garnish

Heat the olive oil in a skillet over medium heat. Add 1 teaspoon basil, the garlic and oregano. Sauté lightly for 3 to 5 minutes, watching carefully to prevent the garlic from browning. Add the undrained tomatoes. Sauté for 3 minutes. Add the broth. Increase the heat and bring to a boil. Add the pasta and additional broth if needed to cover the pasta. Cook for 1 to 2 minutes or until the pasta is tender. Remove from the heat. Cover and let stand for 5 to 10 minutes or until the liquid is absorbed. Do not allow the pasta to become too mushy. Sprinkle the cheese over the top and toss to mix. Garnish with fresh basil.

RICH HOLBROOK

Designer Macaroni and Cheese

12 ounces miniature penne
1 teaspoon white truffle oil
2³/4 cups milk
1/4 cup (1/2 stick) butter
1/4 cup all-purpose flour
1 teaspoon salt
1/4 teaspoon white pepper
1/8 teaspoon red pepper
2³/4 cups (11 ounces) shredded
   extra-sharp Cheddar cheese
2/3 cup shredded Gruyère cheese
6 tablespoons shredded
   extra-sharp smoked white
   Cheddar cheese
3 tablespoons minced
   fresh chives
1/4 to 1/2 cup milk
6 tablespoons shredded
   extra-sharp smoked white
   Cheddar cheese
6 tablespoons panko (Japanese
   bread crumbs) or fresh
   bread crumbs
1 tablespoon minced fresh chives
Long strips of fresh chives
   for garnish

Preheat the broiler. Cook the pasta in boiling water in a large saucepan until tender but still firm to the bite, stirring occasionally. Drain and place in a large bowl. Add the truffle oil and toss to coat.

Bring 2³/4 cups milk to a simmer in a medium saucepan over medium-high heat. Remove from the heat. Melt the butter in a large saucepan over medium heat. Add the flour. Cook for 1 minute or until pale golden brown, stirring constantly. Whisk in the hot milk. Cook over medium heat for 2 minutes or until thickened, stirring frequently. Remove from the heat.

Stir in the salt, white pepper and red pepper. Add the extra-sharp Cheddar cheese, Gruyère cheese, 6 tablespoons smoked white Cheddar cheese and 3 tablespoons chives and mix until the cheeses are melted. Add 1/4 to 1/2 cup milk to make of the desired consistency. Add the pasta and toss to coat.

Spoon into six soufflé cups. Sprinkle each with 1 tablespoon smoked white Cheddar cheese and 1 tablespoon panko. Sprinkle with 1 tablespoon chives. Broil for 1 minute or until the bread crumbs are golden brown. Garnish with long strips of fresh chives.

WHITNEY HULTS-RICHARTZ

Polenta Rounds with Black-Eyed Peas

SERVES 10

1 (17-ounce) tube refrigerator
   sun-dried tomato polenta
1 (15-ounce) can black-eyed
   peas, drained and rinsed
1/2 cup finely chopped scallions
1/4 cup water
1/4 teaspoon salt
1/4 teaspoon red pepper
1/2 cup finely chopped tomatoes
1/4 cup fresh cilantro, chopped
Sour cream
Chopped fresh cilantro
   for garnish

Preheat the oven to warm. Cut the polenta into ten even slices. Place in a large nonstick skillet coated with nonstick cooking spray. Cook over medium heat for 5 to 10 minutes on each side or until light brown and crispy. Remove from the heat. Arrange on a baking sheet and place in the oven to keep warm.

Cook the black-eyed peas, scallions, water, salt and red pepper in a skillet over medium heat until the water evaporates. Remove from the heat. Stir in the tomatoes and 1/4 cup cilantro. Spoon over the warm polenta slices and top with a dollop of sour cream. Arrange on a serving platter and sprinkle with cilantro.

Apalachicola Oyster Bake

SERVES 8

1 slice bacon
1/2 cup (1 stick) butter
1 cup chopped onion
1 (8-ounce) package herb stuffing
1 cup sour cream
1 (10-ounce) can cream of
   mushroom soup, or 1 cup
   Simple Cream of Mushroom
   Soup (page 48)
1 (14-ounce) can tomatoes
1 cup (4 ounces) shredded sharp
   Cheddar cheese
1/2 cup chopped celery
1/2 cup chopped green
   bell pepper
1/2 teaspoon horseradish
1 pint oysters, drained
1 green bell pepper, cut into rings
   for garnish

Preheat the oven to 350 degrees. Fry the bacon in a large skillet until crisp. Remove the bacon to paper towels to drain. Add the butter to the bacon drippings and heat until melted. Add the onion and sauté until translucent. Stir in the stuffing. Combine the sour cream and soup in a bowl. Add the tomatoes, cheese, celery, chopped bell pepper, horseradish and oysters. Spread one-half of the stuffing mixture in the bottom of a 9×13-inch baking dish. Pour the oyster mixture over the stuffing. Spread the remaining stuffing mixture over the top. Crumble the bacon over the layers and top with the bell pepper rings. Bake for 1 hour.

ORIGINALLY PUBLISHED IN *Thymes Remembered*

LIGHTEN UP

By taking advantage of readily available reduced-fat products, this recipe can be nutritionally shaped up quite easily. Reduce the butter by half, use reduced-fat or fat-free sour cream, and choose healthier canned soups for a tasty but heart-healthy dish.

Rosemary Polenta

1/2 cup (1 stick) unsalted butter

1/4 cup extra-virgin olive oil

3 garlic cloves, minced

1 teaspoon crushed red
   pepper flakes

1 teaspoon plus 1 pinch
   fresh rosemary

1 teaspoon kosher salt

1/2 teaspoon freshly ground
   black pepper

3 cups chicken stock

2 cups half-and-half

2 cups milk

2 cups cornmeal

1/2 cup (2 ounces) good-quality
   grated Parmesan cheese

1/4 cup all-purpose flour

1 tablespoon butter

1 tablespoon extra-virgin olive oil

Heat 1/2 cup butter and 1/4 cup olive oil in a large saucepan. Add the garlic, red pepper flakes, rosemary, kosher salt and black pepper and sauté for 1 minute. Add the chicken stock, half-and-half and milk. Bring to a boil and remove from the heat. Whisk in the cornmeal gradually. Cook over low heat for a few minutes or until thickened and bubbly, stirring constantly. Remove from the heat. Stir in the cheese. Pour into a 9×13-inch pan and smooth the top. Chill until firm and cold.

Cut the polenta into twelve squares. Lift each square out with a spatula and cut diagonally into triangles. Sprinkle each triangle lightly with the flour. Heat 1 tablespoon butter and 1 tablespoon olive oil in a large sauté pan. Cook the triangles in batches in the hot butter mixture over medium heat for 3 to 5 minutes or until brown and heated through, turning once and adding additional butter and olive oil as needed. Serve immediately or cover and keep warm in a 150-degree oven until serving time.

LIBBY BIGHAM

Rich Corn Rice

1 (5-ounce) package yellow rice

1 tablespoon butter

2 tablespoons all-purpose flour

3/4 cup cream

3/4 cup chicken broth

1/4 cup (1 ounce) shredded
   Mexican cheese blend

1 (11-ounce) can Mexicorn

2 tablespoons butter,
   cut into cubes

1/2 teaspoon salt

Preheat the oven to 350 degrees. Cook the rice in a medium saucepan using the package directions for 20 minutes. Melt 1 tablespoon butter in a medium saucepan over medium-high heat. Whisk in the flour gradually. Cook for 2 minutes or until smooth, whisking constantly. Whisk in the cream and broth gradually. Add the cheese and remove from the heat. Let stand until the cheese melts, stirring occasionally. Drain the corn and place in a large bowl. Stir in the cubed butter. Add the rice, cheese mixture and salt and mix well. Spoon into a greased 9×13-inch baking dish. Bake for 30 minutes. Serve warm or as a cold dip with blue tortilla chips.

LAURIE D. HARTSFIELD

Rice Pilaf

1/4 cup (1/2 stick) unsalted butter
1 onion, chopped
8 ounces mushrooms, sliced
3/4 cup white rice
1 tablespoon sherry (optional)
2 cups chicken broth
1 bunch scallions, finely chopped

Melt the butter in a large skillet over medium-high heat. Add the onion and mushrooms and sauté until the onion is translucent. Add the rice and sauté for 3 to 5 minutes. Add the sherry and broth. Bring to a boil and reduce the heat to low. Simmer for 30 minutes or until all the liquid is absorbed. Stir in the scallions just before serving.

Wild Rice with Pine Nuts

1 cup long grain and wild
   rice mix
2 cups water
1/2 teaspoon salt
1/3 cup olive oil
2 tomatoes, chopped
1/4 cup pine nuts
1 large green bell pepper, chopped
1/2 cup chopped scallions
1/2 cup (2 ounces) shredded
   Monterey Jack cheese
   with peppers
1/2 cup (2 ounces) shredded sharp
   Cheddar cheese
1/4 cup fresh cilantro, minced

Bring the rice mix, water and salt to a boil in a medium saucepan and reduce the heat. Cover and simmer until the rice is tender. Remove from the heat to cool thoroughly. Combine the cooked rice, olive oil, tomatoes, pine nuts, bell pepper, scallions, cheeses and cilantro in a large bowl and mix well. Chill, covered, in the refrigerator.

ORIGINALLY PUBLISHED IN *Finding Thyme*

TALLAHASSEE TIDBIT

The Marching 100 band from Florida Agricultural & Mechanical University was the only American group invited to perform in France's bicentennial celebration in 1989. The band also performed during the 2009 inauguration of President Barack Obama. The band has been featured on numerous television shows and commercials.

Parmesan Goat Cheese Biscuits

SERVES 8

2 cups self-rising flour
2 teaspoons baking powder
1/2 teaspoon baking soda
1 teaspoon salt
1/4 cup (1/2 stick) cold butter
1/4 cup goat cheese
1 cup buttermilk
1 tablespoon butter
Melted butter for brushing
1/4 cup (1 ounce) grated
    Parmesan cheese

Preheat the oven to 425 degrees. Place a 10-inch cast-iron skillet in the oven to preheat. Mix the flour, baking powder, baking soda and salt in a medium bowl. Cut in 1/4 cup butter and the goat cheese until crumbly. Make a well in the center. Add the buttermilk and stir until moistened, adding an additional tablespoon of buttermilk if needed.

Place 1 tablespoon butter in the hot skillet and let stand until melted. Drop the batter by 1/4 cupfuls into the butter. Brush the tops of the biscuits with melted butter. Bake for 14 to 16 minutes or until brown. Remove from the oven and sprinkle with Parmesan cheese.

CHEF ART SMITH

Broccoli Corn Bread

SERVES 8 TO 10

2 (8-ounce) packages corn
    muffin mix
4 eggs
12 ounces whipped cottage cheese
3/4 cup (1 1/2 sticks) butter, melted
1 (10-ounce) package frozen
    chopped broccoli, thawed
1 onion, finely chopped

Preheat the oven to 350 degrees. Mix the corn muffin mix in a large bowl to remove any lumps. Beat the eggs in a large bowl. Add the cottage cheese and butter and mix well. Stir in the corn muffin mix just until moistened. Fold in the broccoli and onion. Spoon into a greased 9×13-inch baking pan.

Bake for 40 to 45 minutes or until the top is light brown. Let stand for 10 minutes before serving. Serve warm.

Store any leftovers in the refrigerator. If you are unable find whipped cottage cheese, process regular cottage cheese in a food processor until smooth.

CALYNNE HILL

Gorgonzola-Stuffed Bread

1 (1-pound) loaf French bread
1 tablespoon olive oil
6 cups sliced assorted mushrooms
1 cup sliced scallions
2 garlic cloves, minced
1 cup crumbled
　Gorgonzola cheese

Preheat the oven to 400 degrees. Split the bread into halves lengthwise. Scoop out the center of each half leaving shells 1 inch thick. Heat a large skillet over medium-high heat. Spoon the olive oil into the hot skillet. Add the mushrooms, scallions and garlic and sauté until tender and most of the liquid has evaporated. Spoon into the bottom bread shell. Sprinkle with the cheese and replace the top half of the bread. Wrap in foil. Bake for 15 to 20 minutes or until the cheese melts. Unwrap and cut crosswise into slices. Serve warm.

SAUCY CATERING

Cheesy Ciabatta

1 loaf ciabatta
1/4 cup (1/2 stick) butter
3 garlic cloves, minced
1 teaspoon finely chopped fresh
　Italian flat-leaf parsley
1/2 cup (2 ounces) grated
　Parmesan cheese
1 1/2 cups (6 ounces) shredded
　mozzarella cheese

Preheat the oven to 300 degrees. Cut the bread into halves lengthwise and place on a baking sheet. Melt the butter with the garlic in a small saucepan over medium heat. Brush over the bread and sprinkle with the parsley. Sprinkle with the Parmesan cheese and layer the mozzarella cheese over the top. Bake until the cheese is bubbly. For an easy appetizer, cut the bread into small squares and serve with marinara sauce or Tomato Sauce (page 72).

Sausage and Peppers Bread

1 (1-pound) loaf Italian sandwich
bread dough or pizza dough ball

1 (12-ounce) package precooked
spinach and feta chicken
sausage, or 12 ounces Italian
pork sausage

$1/3$ cup finely chopped onion

1 teaspoon oregano

1 teaspoon basil

1 garlic clove, minced

2 cups (8 ounces) shredded
mozzarella cheese

2 tablespoons freshly grated
good-quality Parmigiano-
Reggiano cheese

$1/2$ red bell pepper,
finely chopped

$1/2$ yellow bell pepper,
finely chopped

$1/2$ orange bell pepper,
finely chopped

1 or 2 egg whites

1 tablespoon sesame seeds

Preheat the oven to 400 degrees. Roll the dough on a lightly floured surface with a rolling pin into a 15-inch square. Cover with a towel and let stand until doubled in bulk.

Remove the casing from the sausage. Pulse the sausage in a food processor until crumbly. If you are using Italian pork sausage, cook in a skillet over medium-high heat until cooked through.

Spread the onion over the dough. Sprinkle the oregano, basil and garlic over the onion. Sprinkle the mozzarella cheese and Parmigiano-Reggiano cheese evenly over the herbs. Layer the sausage over the cheese. Top with the bell peppers. Roll up to enclose the filling. Place seam side down on a baking sheet and fashion into a "U" shape. Brush the entire roll-up with egg whites. Sprinkle the sesame seeds over the top. Bake for 20 minutes or until golden brown and cooked through.

DARCY BYINGTON

Bakes

(bāk•s)

1. Prepared to perfection with dry heat,
especially in an oven;
family favorites and crowd pleasers.

Artichoke Chicken Casserole

3 whole chicken breasts, cut into
   halves, skinned and boned
Salt and lemon pepper to taste
All-purpose flour for dredging
Extra-virgin olive oil for browning
2 bunches scallions, chopped
1 green bell pepper, chopped
1 (14-ounce) can water-pack
   artichoke hearts
1 pound fresh mushrooms, sliced
3 cups chicken stock
1 pint cherry tomatoes,
   cut into halves
$^{1}/_{2}$ cup parsley, chopped
1 (10-ounce) package yellow
   rice mix

Preheat the oven to 350 degrees. Sprinkle the chicken with salt and lemon pepper. Dredge in flour to coat. Brown the chicken in olive oil in a skillet. Remove to paper towels to drain. Sauté the scallions and bell pepper in the drippings in the skillet. Add the artichoke hearts and mushrooms. Add 1 cup of the chicken stock and the tomatoes.

Arrange the chicken in a 3-quart baking dish. Pour the vegetable mixture over the chicken. Sprinkle with the parsley. Bake, covered with foil, for 40 to 45 minutes or until the chicken is cooked through. Prepare the rice using the package directions, substituting the remaining chicken stock for the water. Serve the chicken over the rice.

ORIGINALLY PUBLISHED IN *Thymes Remembered*

Photograph for this recipe appears on page 80.

Chicken Casserole Olé

1 (10-ounce) can cream of
   mushroom soup, or $^{3}/_{4}$ cup
   Simple Cream of Mushroom
   Soup (page 48)
1 cup sour cream
1 white onion, chopped
1 (6-ounce) can sliced black
   olives, drained
Crushed nacho chips
4 cooked chicken breasts, shredded
1 cup (4 ounces) shredded mild
   Cheddar cheese
Fresh salsa

Preheat the oven to 350 degrees. Mix the soup, sour cream, onion and olives in a bowl. Line a 9×13-inch baking dish with crushed nacho chips. Layer the chicken, soup mixture and cheese one-half at a time over the nacho chips. Bake for 30 to 40 minutes or until heated through. Serve with fresh salsa on the side.

SARA BAYLISS

Chicken and Broccoli Casserole

1 (14-ounce) package frozen chopped broccoli, thawed

3 to 4 cups chopped fried chicken fingers or cooked chicken breasts (about 4)

1 cup mayonnaise

1 (10-ounce) can cream of mushroom soup, or 3/4 cup Simple Cream of Mushroom Soup (page 48)

1 (10-ounce) can cream of chicken soup

1 teaspoon lemon juice

1/2 teaspoon curry powder (optional)

1 cup (4 ounces) shredded Cheddar cheese

1 teaspoon hot red pepper sauce

1 cup crumbled butter crackers

Butter for topping

Hot cooked rice

Preheat the oven to 375 degrees. Layer the broccoli and chicken in a buttered 9×13-inch baking dish. Mix the mayonnaise, mushroom soup, chicken soup, lemon juice, curry powder, cheese and hot sauce in a saucepan.

Heat until smooth, stirring frequently. Pour evenly over the chicken. Top with the crackers and dot with butter. Bake for 20 minutes. Serve with rice.

NANCY CLICK

LIGHTEN UP

Casseroles or "bakes" are great make-ahead options for those busy days in our lives. They typically contain creams, cheeses, and mayonnaise, which all lend themselves to more healthy substitutions. Use skinless chicken breasts and reduced-fat mayonnaise, soups, and butter crackers in this recipe to benefit from significant fat reductions.

Chicken Spinach Bake

8 ounces bow tie pasta

1 cup finely chopped onion

1 tablespoon olive oil

1 (10-ounce) package frozen chopped spinach, thawed

3 cups cubed cooked chicken breasts (4 breasts)

1 (14-ounce) can Italian-style diced tomatoes

8 ounces tub-style chive and onion cream cheese

1 tablespoon Accent

1/2 teaspoon crushed red pepper

Salt and black pepper to taste

1 cup (4 ounces) shredded mozzarella cheese

Preheat the oven to 375 degrees. Cook the pasta using the package directions. Drain and set aside. Sauté the onion in the olive oil in a skillet until translucent. Drain the spinach well, pressing between paper towels to absorb any excess moisture.

Combine the chicken, pasta, spinach, tomatoes, sautéed onion, cream cheese, MSG, red pepper, salt and black pepper in a bowl and mix well. Spoon into a 9×13-inch baking dish. Sprinkle evenly with mozzarella cheese. Bake, covered, for 30 minutes. Bake, uncovered, for 15 minutes longer or until bubbly. Serve with salad and garlic bread.

TALLAHASSEE TIDBIT

The 2000 presidential election was decided after a recount headquartered in Tallahassee. After 36 days, the United States Supreme Court halted the recount and declared George W. Bush the winner.

Savory Chicken Potpie

1/3 cup butter

1/2 cup Bisquick

1/3 cup chopped onion

1/4 teaspoon pepper

1/8 teaspoon dried thyme leaves

1 1/2 cups chicken broth

2/3 cup milk

1 3/4 cups chopped rosemary and
   garlic rotisserie chicken

1 (10-ounce) package frozen
   mixed vegetables

1 1/2 cups Bisquick

2 teaspoons sesame seeds, poppy
   seeds or celery seeds

3 tablespoons hot water

3 tablespoons butter, softened

Preheat the oven to 425 degrees. Heat 1/3 cup butter in a 2-quart saucepan over low heat until melted. Stir in 1/2 cup Bisquick, the onion, pepper and thyme. Cook over low heat until bubbly, stirring constantly. Remove from the heat. Stir in the broth and milk. Bring to a boil, stirring constantly. Boil for 1 minute, stirring constantly. Stir in the chicken and mixed vegetables. Cook over low heat for 10 minutes or until heated through. Pour into a lightly greased 9×9-inch baking pan.

Mix 1 1/2 cups Bisquick, the sesame seeds, hot water and 3 tablespoons butter in a bowl to form a soft dough. Shape the dough gently into a smooth ball on a cloth dusted with all-purpose flour or baking mix on a counter or table. Knead the dough five times.

Roll or pat the dough into a 9-inch square. Place over the chicken mixture. Cut at least three vents in the center to allow steam to escape. Bake for 20 to 25 minutes or until the crust is deep golden brown.

The chicken mixture can be prepared the night before. Be sure to reheat before pouring into the baking pan.

SANDY CROCKETT

Chicken Tetrazzini

1/4 cup (1/2 stick) butter
1/4 cup all-purpose flour
1 teaspoon salt
1/4 teaspoon pepper
1 cup milk
1 (4-ounce) can black
   olives, drained
4 ounces sliced mushrooms
1/4 cup sherry
20 ounces spaghetti
Salt to taste
1 1/2 pounds cooked chicken,
   chopped or cubed
8 ounces sharp Cheddar
   cheese, shredded
1 (2-ounce) package
   chopped almonds

Preheat the oven to 350 degrees. Melt the butter in a saucepan over medium-high heat. Add the flour and mix well. Add 1 teaspoon salt and the pepper. Cook for 3 minutes. Add the milk gradually, stirring constantly. Cook for 15 minutes or to a cream sauce consistency, stirring frequently. Stir in the olives, mushrooms and wine. Cook the spaghetti in salted water in a large saucepan until al dente; drain.

Alternate layers of the spaghetti, chicken and sauce in a 9×13-inch baking dish until all ingredients are used. Sprinkle the cheese and almonds evenly over the top. Bake until bubbly.

For variation, one 10-ounce can cream of mushroom soup or 1/2 cup Simple Cream of Mushroom Soup on page 48 may be used instead of the mushrooms for a more creamy texture. The spaghetti may be cooked in chicken broth for more chicken flavor.

JEAN McCULLY

Chicken and Rice Casserole

1 (6-ounce) package Uncle Ben's
   long grain and wild rice
   original recipe with 23 herbs
   and seasonings
3 cups shredded cooked chicken
2 (14-ounce) cans French-style
   green beans, drained
1 (8-ounce) can water
   chestnuts, chopped
1 (10-ounce) can cream of
   mushroom soup, or 3/4 cup
   Simple Cream of Mushroom
   Soup (page 48)
1 cup mayonnaise
1 onion, chopped
1 (4-ounce) jar pimentos (optional)

Prepare the rice mix using the package directions. Preheat the oven to 350 degrees. Combine the prepared rice with the chicken, green beans, water chestnuts, soup, mayonnaise, onion and pimentos in a large bowl and mix well. Spoon into a 9×13-inch baking dish. Bake for 30 minutes. Cool for 10 minutes.

MARIANNE BROOKS

Mushroom and Turkey Sausage Lasagna

12 ounces ground Italian sausage,
  casings removed

8 ounces ground turkey

8 ounces sliced mushrooms

1/2 cup chopped onion

1 (26-ounce) jar basil and tomato
  sauce, or 31/4 cups Tomato
  Sauce (page 72)

32 ounces low-fat ricotta cheese

1 egg, beaten

2 teaspoons Italian seasoning

1 tablespoon grated
  Parmesan cheese

1/4 teaspoon salt

10 uncooked whole wheat
  lasagna noodles

4 cups (16 ounces) shredded
  mozzarella cheese

Preheat the oven to 375 degrees. Cook the sausage and ground turkey in a skillet sprayed with nonstick cooking spray until no longer pink, stirring until crumbly. Add the mushrooms and onion. Cook for 3 to 5 minutes or until the onion is translucent; drain. Stir in the sauce. Mix the ricotta cheese, egg, seasoning, Parmesan cheese and salt in a large bowl until blended.

Layer the uncooked noodles, ground turkey mixture, ricotta cheese mixture and mozzarella cheese one-half at a time in a lightly greased 9×13-inch baking dish. Bake, covered, for 55 minutes. Bake, uncovered, for 10 to 15 minutes or until bubbly. Let stand for 10 to 15 minutes before serving.

CALYNNE HILL

LIGHTEN UP

The addition of whole wheat lasagna noodles to supermarket shelves gives us the choice for more fiber and phytochemicals while still providing an excellent, complex carbohydrate energy option. If whole wheat pasta is a new addition to your dinner table, take it slowly initially by mixing it with regular pasta. Making the switch to whole grain takes a little time but is well worth the effort.

Hot Italian Lasagna

8 or 9 hot Italian sausage links
1 pound lean ground beef
1 large yellow onion,
  finely chopped
1/2 to 1 green bell pepper, chopped
2 tablespoons Italian seasoning
1 teaspoon pepper
1 (16-ounce) can chopped
  tomatoes
1 (16-ounce) can tomato sauce
1 cup water
1 (8-ounce) can tomato paste
1 teaspoon sugar
10 to 15 cups water
1 tablespoon olive oil
Dash of salt
1 (16-ounce) package
  lasagna noodles
2 1/2 cups (10 ounces) shredded
  mozzarella cheese
1 1/2 cups (6 ounces) grated
  Parmesan cheese

Remove the casings from the sausage. Cut the sausage into bite-size pieces. Brown the sausage and ground beef in a large skillet over medium-high heat, stirring until crumbly; drain. Add the onion, bell pepper, Italian seasoning and pepper. Cook for 10 minutes.

Add the tomatoes, tomato sauce and 1 cup water. Bring to a boil. Stir in the tomato paste and sugar. Return to a boil. Cover and reduce the heat to low. Simmer for 4 to 6 hours, stirring at least once every 30 minutes.

Preheat the oven to 375 degrees. Bring 10 to 15 cups water to a boil in a large stockpot. Add the olive oil and salt. Add the lasagna noodles. Cook for 2 minutes less than the package directions; drain. Mix the mozzarella cheese and Parmesan cheese in a bowl.

Spread 1/2 cup of the sauce in a 9×13-inch glass baking dish. Alternate layers of the lasagna noodles, the remaining sauce and the cheese mixture in the prepared dish, ending with the cheese mixture. Bake for 30 to 45 minutes or until lightly browned on top. Let cool for 15 minutes or longer before slicing to serve.

KENDRA H. HOWARD

Spinach Lasagna

1 onion, chopped

¹/4 cup (¹/2 stick) butter

4 garlic cloves, minced

2 (10-ounce) packages frozen
   spinach, thawed and
   well drained

¹/2 teaspoon nutmeg

1 teaspoon salt

¹/4 teaspoon red pepper

1 tablespoon Italian seasoning

1¹/2 cups cottage cheese

1¹/2 cups part-skim ricotta cheese

³/4 cup (3 ounces) grated
   Parmesan cheese

2 cups (8 ounces) shredded
   mozzarella cheese

2 eggs, beaten

¹/4 cup chopped fresh parsley

5 cups marinara sauce, or 5 cups
   Tomato Sauce (page 72)

³/4 cup heavy cream

1 tablespoon extra-virgin olive oil

1 package no-cook
   lasagna noodles

³/4 cup (3 ounces) grated
   Parmesan cheese

Preheat the oven to 350 degrees. Sauté the onion in the butter in a medium skillet over medium-high heat for 15 minutes. Add the garlic. Sauté for 3 to 5 minutes. Add the spinach, nutmeg, salt, red pepper and Italian seasoning. Sauté for 5 minutes. Remove from the heat to cool.

Combine the cottage cheese, ricotta cheese, ³/4 cup Parmesan cheese, the mozzarella cheese, eggs and parsley in a large mixing bowl and mix well. Fold in the spinach mixture. Blend the marinara sauce and cream in a medium bowl.

Grease the bottom and sides of a 9×13-inch baking dish with the olive oil. Spread a thin layer of the creamy marinara sauce in the prepared baking dish. Arrange a layer of the noodles over the creamy marinara sauce. Layer one-third of the spinach mixture, 1 cup of the creamy marinara sauce and another layer of the remaining noodles over the noodles. Repeat the layers twice, ending with the creamy marinara sauce. Sprinkle with ³/4 cup Parmesan cheese. Bake, covered with foil, for 40 minutes. Bake, uncovered, for 10 minutes longer. Let stand for 10 minutes before serving.

Zingy Lasagna

2 tablespoons extra-virgin
   olive oil
1 pound lean ground beef
1 large can refried beans
2 teaspoons oregano
1 teaspoon ground cumin
3/4 teaspoon garlic powder
12 uncooked lasagna noodles
1 tablespoon extra-virgin olive oil
2 1/2 cups salsa
2 1/2 cups water
3/4 cup chopped scallions
1 (6-ounce) can sliced black
   olives, drained and rinsed
2 cups sour cream
1 cup (4 ounces) shredded
   Monterey Jack cheese

Preheat the oven to 350 degrees. Heat 2 tablespoons olive oil in a large skillet over medium heat. Add the ground beef. Cook for 5 minutes or until brown, stirring until crumbly; drain. Add the beans, oregano, cumin and garlic powder and mix well. Soak the lasagna noodles in water to cover in a large stockpot for 5 minutes.

Coat a 9×13-inch baking dish with 1 tablespoon olive oil. Layer one-third of the lasagna noodles, one-half of the ground beef mixture, one-half of the remaining lasagna noodles, the remaining ground beef mixture and the remaining lasagna noodles in the prepared dish.

Mix the salsa with 2 1/2 cups water and pour over the layers. Bake, covered with foil, for 1 hour and 30 minutes. Mix the scallions, olives, sour cream and cheese in a bowl. Uncover the lasagna and spread the sour cream mixture evenly over the top. Bake, uncovered, for 5 minutes. Garnish with additional salsa.

SARA BAYLISS

LIGHTEN UP

This recipe also can be a delightful meatless meal by adding a can of black beans in place of the ground beef. Choose the fat-free refried beans as many canned refried beans have added lard. Substitute lower-fat sour cream and reduced-fat cheese, and leave out the olive oil altogether for a healthier nutritional profile.

Sausage and Wine Pasta Bake

1 tablespoon extra-virgin olive oil

1 cup finely chopped onion

3 garlic cloves, minced

1/2 teaspoon salt

1/2 teaspoon pepper

1 pound ground Italian sausage

1 (10-ounce) package frozen spinach, cooked, drained and squeezed to remove excess moisture

1/2 cup cabernet sauvignon

8 ounces cream cheese, softened

2 cups marinara sauce, or 2 cups Tomato Sauce (page 72)

8 ounces ziti

Salt to taste

2 cups (8 ounces) shredded Italian cheese blend

Preheat the oven to 375 degrees. Spread the olive oil in a 9×13-inch baking dish. Add the onion, garlic, 1/2 teaspoon salt and the pepper and mix well. Bake for 15 minutes. Remove from the oven and spoon into a large bowl. Set the baking dish aside.

Brown the sausage in a large skillet over medium-high heat for 8 to 10 minutes, stirring until crumbly. Drain the sausage and return to low heat. Add the spinach and wine and mix well. Add the cream cheese. Heat until melted, stirring constantly. Remove from the heat. Add the onion mixture. Stir in the marinara sauce.

Cook the pasta in boiling salted water using the package directions; drain. Add to the sausage mixture and toss to mix. Place in the baking dish. Sprinkle with the Italian cheese. Bake, covered, for 30 minutes. Bake, uncovered, for 15 minutes longer.

APRIL JOHNSTON

THYME SAVER

Using alcoholic beverages in your cooking can often add a great deal of flavor. However, keep in mind when using beer, wine or liquor in recipes, much of the alcohol remains after cooking. If this is a concern, you may be able to substitute fruit juices or chicken or beef stock.

Tortellini with Prosciutto Sage Cream Sauce

SERVES 4

Pinch of salt
1 (20-ounce) package tortellini or chicken herb tortellini
1/4 cup (1/2 stick) butter
2 tablespoons all-purpose flour, sifted
2 cups cream
1 cup milk
1 teaspoon salt
1 teaspoon dried rubbed sage
1 cup (4 ounces) grated good-quality Parmesan cheese
4 slices prosciutto, finely chopped (about 3 ounces)
1/2 cup baby sweet peas

Fill a medium saucepan three-fourths full of water. Add a pinch of salt. Bring to a boil over high heat. Add the pasta. Cook for 8 minutes.

Melt the butter in a medium saucepan over medium-high heat. Whisk in the flour until smooth. Cook for 2 minutes, whisking constantly. Whisk in the cream and milk gradually. Add 1 teaspoon salt, the sage and cheese. Cook for 3 minutes or until the cheese melts, whisking constantly. Remove from the heat. Stir in the prosciutto and peas. Drain the pasta. Add the sauce and toss to coat. Serve immediately.

GINA COLLEY-HOLGATE

Creamy Rigatoni Bake

SERVES 8 TO 10

1/2 Vidalia onion or other sweet onion, chopped
2 tablespoons salted butter
2 pounds ground sirloin
1 1/2 teaspoons meat seasoning blend, or 1 1/2 teaspoons Italian seasoning plus 1 1/2 teaspoons paprika
1 (26-ounce) jar marinara sauce, or 3 1/4 cups Tomato Sauce (page 72)
16 ounces rigatoni
8 ounces cream cheese
1 cup sour cream
1/4 cup (1/2 stick) salted butter
1 1/2 cups (6 ounces) shredded sharp Cheddar cheese

Preheat the oven to 350 degrees. Sauté the onion in 2 tablespoons butter in a skillet for 5 minutes. Add the ground sirloin and meat seasoning blend. Cook until the ground sirloin is brown, stirring until crumbly; drain. Stir in the marinara sauce. Simmer for 20 minutes.

Cook the pasta using the package directions; drain. Mix the cream cheese, sour cream and 1/4 cup butter in a large saucepan. Cook until melted, stirring constantly. Add the pasta and toss to coat well. Pour into a greased 9×13-inch baking dish. Layer the ground sirloin sauce over the pasta. Sprinkle the Cheddar cheese over the top. Bake, uncovered, for 30 minutes or until bubbly.

KARA COLLEY

Spaghetti Pie

6 ounces vermicelli
2 tablespoons butter
1/3 cup grated Parmesan cheese
2 eggs, well beaten
8 ounces ground beef
1 (10-ounce) jar marinara sauce,
    or 1 1/4 cups Tomato Sauce
    (page 72)
3/4 teaspoon dried oregano
1 cup cottage cheese
1/2 cup (2 ounces) shredded
    mozzarella cheese
10 pepperoni slices,
    cut into quarters

Preheat the oven to 350 degrees. Cook the pasta using the package directions. Drain and return to the saucepan. Add the butter and Parmesan cheese and toss well. Add the eggs and mix well. Spoon into a greased 10-inch pie plate and shape into a shell. Bake, uncovered, for 9 minutes or until set.

Brown the ground beef in a large skillet, stirring until crumbly. Drain and return to the skillet. Stir in the marinara sauce and oregano. Cook over medium heat for 10 minutes, stirring occasionally. Spread the cottage cheese evenly over the pasta shell and spoon the ground beef mixture over the top.

Bake, covered with foil, for 15 minutes. Sprinkle with the mozzarella cheese. Top with the pepperoni. Bake, uncovered, for 5 minutes or until the cheese melts. Remove from the oven and let stand for 10 minutes before serving.

CARLA ANNE GASKIN

LIGHTEN UP

This recipe easily lends itself to increased fiber by using whole wheat pasta. Leave out the butter and pepperoni to elevate the nutritional profile even more.

Cabbage and Ground Beef Casserole   SERVES 8 TO 10

1 tablespoon vegetable oil
1 pound ground beef or spicy
    bulk pork sausage
2 green bell peppers, chopped
1 onion, chopped
2 garlic cloves, minced
1 (10-ounce) can diced tomatoes
    with green chiles
1 (8-ounce) can tomato sauce
1/2 cup uncooked white or
    brown rice
1 teaspoon salt
1/2 teaspoon dried basil
1/2 teaspoon dried oregano
1/4 teaspoon cayenne pepper
1/4 teaspoon black pepper
1 small head cabbage, chopped
1 cup (4 ounces) shredded
    Colby cheese

Preheat the oven to 350 degrees. Heat the oil in a large skillet over medium heat. Add the ground beef, bell peppers, onion and garlic. Cook for 8 minutes or until the ground beef is brown and the vegetables are soft, stirring until the ground beef is crumbly; drain. Stir in the undrained tomatoes with green chiles, tomato sauce, rice, salt, basil, oregano, cayenne pepper and black pepper. Adjust the black pepper to taste.

Spread in an ungreased 9×13-inch baking dish. Layer the cabbage and cheese over the top. Bake, covered, for 65 to 75 minutes or until the rice is tender, uncovering during the last 10 minutes. Serve with fresh garlic bread.

SARA J. MARCHESSAULT

Tortilla Pie

1 pound lean ground beef or
  ground turkey
1 cup chopped yellow onion
1 garlic clove, minced
1 (4-ounce) can diced green
  chiles, drained
1 (8-ounce) can no-salt-added
  tomato sauce
1/2 teaspoon salt
Freshly ground pepper to taste
4 corn tortillas, cut into halves
2 cups (8 ounces) shredded
  Pepper Jack cheese
1 cup pitted black olives
  for garnish
Sour cream for garnish

Preheat the oven to 350 degrees. Brown the ground beef with the onion and garlic in a large nonstick skillet for 5 to 6 minutes or until the onion is tender, stirring until the ground beef is crumbly; drain. Add the green chiles, tomato sauce, salt and pepper and mix well. Simmer for a few minutes to meld the flavors.

Line an 8-inch deep-dish pie plate coated with nonstick cooking spray with one-half of the tortilla halves. Do not worry about the overlap. Layer one-half of the ground beef sauce and one-half of the cheese over the tortilla halves. Repeat the layers. Bake, covered with foil, for 20 to 25 minutes or until bubbly. Let stand for 5 to 10 minutes before serving. Cut into six wedges and garnish with the olives and sour cream.

CINDY WISE

Buttery Blue Shrimp

2 pounds (20- to 25-count)
  uncooked shrimp, peeled
  and deveined
Juice of 2 limes
1/2 cup (1 stick) butter, melted
6 ounces cream cheese
2 ounces blue cheese
8 ounces bow tie pasta
1 tablespoon butter, melted
Fresh lemon juice to taste
Chopped fresh parsley to taste

Preheat the oven to 400 degrees. Arrange the shrimp in a baking dish and sprinkle with the lime juice. Melt 1/2 cup butter, the cream cheese and blue cheese in a heavy skillet over low heat, stirring constantly. Pour over the shrimp. Bake for 20 minutes.

Prepare the pasta using the package directions. Drain and place in a large serving bowl. Add 1 tablespoon melted butter, the lemon juice and parsley and toss to coat. Pour the shrimp mixture over the pasta. Serve immediately. To serve as an appetizer, eliminate the pasta, chop the shrimp and serve with crackers.

MONICA BROWNING

En·trées

(on'•trā)

1. The centerpiece of a meal;
delivers comfort and smiles.

Orange Basil Salmon

1/4 cup orange juice

2 tablespoons lemon juice

2 tablespoons olive oil

1/3 cup chopped fresh basil

2 tablespoons grated orange zest

4 (1-inch-thick) salmon fillets or salmon steaks

Preheat the grill. Mix the orange juice, lemon juice, olive oil, basil and orange zest in a bowl. Place the fish in a shallow dish or in a sealable plastic bag. Pour the marinade over the fish. Cover the dish or seal the bag. Marinate in the refrigerator for 2 hours. Remove the fish from the marinade and place on a lightly greased grill rack. Grill, covered with the grill lid, for 10 minutes on each side or until the fish flakes easily with a fork.

LAURIE D. HARTSFIELD

Photograph for this recipe appears on page 96.

WINE PAIRING
Serve with a dry French rosé that has enough body for the salmon yet is light with its rosé qualities, sweet strawberry, and bracing tannins.

LIGHTEN UP
When it comes to health benefits, fish continue to line up high on the positive side. Fish is an excellent lean protein source and is rich in essential vitamins and minerals. It provides a good source of the fatty acid omega-3, which can help reduce the risk of heart attacks. Limit the olive oil and enjoy a tasty, highly nutritious, and low-fat dish.

Garlic-Rubbed Black Grouper with Kalamata Olive Coulis and Pinched Herb Salad

SERVES 2

2 (6-ounce) fresh grouper fillets or other firm white fish fillets, skin and bones removed

Salt and pepper to taste

Light olive oil as needed

4 ounces dry white wine

4 ounces low-sodium chicken broth

4 garlic cloves, minced

1 ounce extra-virgin olive oil

1/2 cup drained pitted kalamata olives

1/4 cup mix of coarsely chopped fresh herbs such as parsley, chives and basil

1/4 cup coarsely chopped or torn lettuce

Splash of light-style vinegar or white wine

Preheat the oven to 400 degrees. Heat an ovenproof sauté pan large enough to accommodate both fish fillets over medium-high heat. Sprinkle both sides of the fish with salt and pepper. Place enough light olive oil in the hot sauté pan to lightly coat the bottom. Place the fish carefully in the hot olive oil. Cook for 2 minutes or until a brown crust forms. Turn the fillets carefully with a spatula. Remove from the heat. Add the wine and broth. Spread the garlic evenly over the fillets. Bake for 5 minutes per inch of thickness or until the fish begins to flake. Do not overcook. Remove the fish from the broth and keep warm. Reserve the cooking broth for sauce.

Process 1 ounce extra-virgin olive oil and the olives in a blender or food processor at medium speed for 15 seconds. The mixture may not mix well, but that is okay. Scrape down the side of the container with a rubber spatula. Drizzle in the reserved cooking broth, processing constantly at low speed until the coulis is the smooth consistency of heavy cream.

Combine the herbs and lettuce in a small bowl. Add a splash of vinegar and toss to coat. Sprinkle with salt and pepper.

Drizzle about 1 ounce of the kalamata olive coulis randomly around the center of each serving plate. Place one fillet on each plate and top with a pinch of the herb salad.

CHEF DAVID GWYNN, CYPRESS RESTAURANT

WINE PAIRING
Serve with an unoaked chardonnay or lighter-style pinot noir. For more variety, try an oily German riesling with layers of stony minerality to tame the acidity and a touch of sweetness to offset the salty kalamata olives.

Marinated Grouper Fillets

SERVES 6

6 (6-ounce) grouper fillets
3/4 teaspoon salt
1/4 cup fresh cilantro
1/4 cup chopped onion
1 tablespoon sugar
1 tablespoon finely chopped
   seeded serrano chile
3 tablespoons fresh lime juice
2 tablespoons tequila
2 tablespoons dry white wine
1 tablespoon vegetable oil
1 garlic clove, chopped
Chopped fresh chives for garnish
Lime wedges for garnish

Place the fish in a single layer in a 9×13-inch baking dish and sprinkle with 1/4 teaspoon of the salt. Process the remaining 1/2 teaspoon salt, the cilantro, onion, sugar, chile, lime juice, tequila, wine, oil and garlic in a blender or food processor until smooth. Pour over the fish and turn to coat. Marinate in the refrigerator for 30 minutes, turning once.

Preheat the grill. Drain the fish, discarding the marinade. Place the fish on a grill rack coated with nonstick cooking spray. Grill for 5 minutes on each side or until the fish flakes easily with a fork. Arrange on a serving plate and garnish with chopped fresh chives and lime wedges.

MAYOR JOHN AND MRS. JANE MARKS

 WINE PAIRING
Serve with a dry, grassy California fumé blanc, which is a sauvignon blanc, showing mouthwatering notes of grass, figs, and lemon-lime.

TALLAHASSEE TIDBIT
When Mayor and Mrs. Marks's son, John Marks, Jr., left for college, Mayor Marks took on a new role as head chef. He began to refine his culinary skills and out of this has come wonderful family recipes. This is a family favorite.

Citus Redfish

$2/3$ cup pineapple juice

6 tablespoons extra-virgin
  olive oil

1 tablespoon grated orange zest

1 tablespoon grated fresh ginger

1 teaspoon Tabasco sauce

Salt and pepper to taste

$1/4$ cup sweetened coconut flakes

6 (4- to 6-ounce) redfish fillets or
  tilapia fillets

Whisk the pineapple juice, olive oil, orange zest, ginger, Tabasco sauce, salt, pepper and coconut in a bowl. Place the fish in a single layer in a large baking dish. Pour the pineapple juice mixture evenly over the fish. Marinate, covered, in the refrigerator for 20 minutes or up to 24 hours.

Preheat a charcoal or gas grill to medium. Place the fish on a grill rack and brush the marinade over the fish. Grill for 5 to 10 minutes on each side or until the fish flakes easily with a fork, turning the fish carefully so it does not fall apart. Serve with a summer salad, fresh steamed vegetables, risotto or rice.

For variation, you may eliminate the marinating time and simply bake the fish in the marinade so it absorbs the marinade and takes less time to prepare. For a more citrus flavor, substitute fresh Florida orange juice for the pineapple juice and eliminate the coconut.

DR. CORY COUCH

WINE PAIRING
Serve with a fruity, crisp riesling from California. The sweetness of the wine will balance the spicy hot sauce.

Snapper Augustine

SERVES 2

2 (7-ounce) red snapper fillets
2 teaspoons Cajun
  blackening seasoning
2 teaspoons butter
4 ounces crawfish tail meat
1 garlic clove, minced
1 teaspoon cilantro
2 teaspoons butter
1/2 teaspoon lemon juice
Salt and pepper to taste

Sprinkle the fish with the blackening seasoning. Cook the fish in 2 teaspoons butter in a cast-iron skillet until blackened on each side. Sauté the crawfish, garlic and cilantro in 2 teaspoons butter in a sauté pan until the crawfish is cooked through. Add the lemon juice, salt and pepper. Spread over the fish and serve.

CHEF GRANT BEANE, GEORGIO'S

WINE PAIRING
The perfect wine for this dish is Pine Ridge's Chenin Blanc-Viognier blend. It features grassy herbs with melon, citrus notes, and just enough fruit to balance with the spicy character of the dish.

Pan-Seared Tuna with Ginger Cream Sauce

SERVES 6

6 (6-ounce) tuna steaks,
  about 1 inch thick
Pepper to taste
2 tablespoons peanut oil or
  canola oil
1/4 cup (1/2 stick) butter
1/3 cup thinly sliced scallions
1/4 cup cilantro, chopped
3 tablespoons finely chopped
  fresh ginger
4 garlic cloves, chopped
7 ounces mushrooms, sliced
5 tablespoons soy sauce
11/2 cups whipping cream
3 tablespoons fresh lime juice
Lime wedges for garnish
Sprigs of fresh cilantro for garnish

Sprinkle one side of the fish with pepper. Heat the peanut oil in a heavy skillet over high heat. Place the fish pepper side down in the hot oil. Sear for 2 minutes. Turn and cook to the desired degree of doneness. Remove to a baking sheet and keep warm. Add the butter, scallions, cilantro, ginger and garlic to the drippings in the skillet. Cook for 30 seconds or until fragrant. Stir in the mushrooms and soy sauce. Simmer for 30 seconds. Add the whipping cream. Simmer until the sauce lightly coats the back of a spoon. Stir in the lime juice. Spoon the sauce onto serving plates and place the fish over the sauce. Garnish with lime wedges and sprigs of cilantro.

ORIGINALLY PUBLISHED IN *Finding Thyme*

WINE PAIRING
Serve with a juicy, delicious California sparkling wine such as Gloria Ferrer Royal Cuvée with its creamy mouth feel and ripe pear fruit with touches of citrus, ginger, and baked apples.

Florida-Style Grilled Fish Tacos

1/4 cup light olive oil
2 garlic cloves, minced
1 tablespoon chili powder
1 teaspoon sea salt
Heavy pinch of pepper
2 pounds favorite firm Florida fish
   such as red snapper, grouper,
   mahimahi, snook, cobia
   or wahoo
12 corn tortillas
1 package shredded
   coleslaw blend
1 small Vidalia onion or other
   sweet onion, sliced
1/2 cup plain yogurt
1/4 cup reduced-fat mayonnaise
Juice of 1/2 lime
Sea salt and pepper to taste
1/2 cup sour cream
   (Mexican-style preferred)
Juice of 2 limes
1/4 cup fresh cilantro, chopped
16 avocado slices
   (about 2 small avocados)
1/4 cup favorite prepared salsa or
   prepare your own
2 limes, cut into wedges
Hot red pepper sauce

Combine the olive oil, garlic, chili powder, 1 teaspoon sea salt and a heavy pinch of pepper. Place the fish in a gallon-size sealable plastic bag. Pour the marinade over the fish and seal the bag. Marinate in the refrigerator for 30 minutes to 4 hours. Drain the fish, discarding the marinade.

Preheat the grill to medium. Place the fish on a grill rack coated well with nonstick cooking spray. Grill for 3 minutes on each side or until the fish flakes easily with a fork. Remove to a platter. Chop the fish into large chunks and cover loosely with foil. Wrap the tortillas in foil. Place on the grill rack and grill for 5 minutes or until heated through.

Toss the coleslaw blend with the onion in a large bowl. Mix the yogurt, mayonnaise and the juice of 1/2 lime in a small bowl. Pour over the coleslaw mixture. Add sea salt and pepper and toss to mix. Chill, covered, in the refrigerator.

Combine the sour cream, juice of 2 limes, one-half of the fresh cilantro, sea salt and pepper and mix well. Chill, covered, in the refrigerator.

Spread a dollop of the lime cream on each tortilla. Top with a piece of fish, a large spoon of coleslaw, the avocado slices, remaining cilantro and some salsa. Serve with the lime wedges, hot sauce and remaining coleslaw.

CHEF JOSH BUTLER, FLORIDA GOVERNOR'S MANSION

 WINE PAIRING
Serve with a refreshing unoaked chardonnay showing clean citrus fruit and biting acidity.

Whole Wheat Fried Fish and Roasted Potatoes

ROASTED POTATOES
3 pounds red potatoes
1 yellow onion, chopped
Salt and pepper to taste
3 to 4 tablespoons olive oil

FISH
1 cup whole wheat flour
1 cup buttermilk
1/2 teaspoon Tabasco sauce
1/4 cup finely chopped pecans
1/2 cup whole wheat bread crumbs
Salt and pepper to taste
Extra-virgin olive oil for frying
4 pounds tilapia, cut into 4 fillets
Ketchup for dipping
Mustard for dipping

To prepare the potatoes, preheat the oven to 475 degrees or a convection oven to 375 degrees. Peel the potatoes and cut into 1/2-inch cubes. Place in a ceramic or glass baking dish and add the onion. Sprinkle generously with salt and pepper. Drizzle with the olive oil and toss until all of the potatoes are coated evenly. Bake, covered, for 30 to 35 minutes or until the potatoes are cooked through, stirring halfway through.

To prepare the fish, place the whole wheat flour in a shallow dish. Mix the buttermilk and Tabasco sauce in a shallow dish. Mix the pecans, bread crumbs, salt and pepper in a shallow dish. Coat the bottom of a large skillet with extra-virgin olive oil and heat over medium-high heat. Coat one fillet in the whole wheat flour and shake to remove any excess flour. Dip into the buttermilk mixture and then dredge in the pecan mixture to coat. Repeat with the remaining fillets. Fry in the hot oil for 3 minutes on each side or until golden brown and the fish flakes easily with a fork, turning when the coating is firm. Dip in ketchup and mustard for additional flavor.

PETER AND KENSY BOULWARE

WINE PAIRING
Serve with chardonnay that has concentrated fruit, cedary oak, and supple buttery tannins with vanilla notes.

TALLAHASSEE TIDBIT
Football legend Peter Boulware was an All-America linebacker for Florida State University from 1993 to 1997, where he met his wife, Kensy, a Seminole volleyball player. Peter went on to become a four-time Pro Bowl player and Super Bowl Champion with the Baltimore Ravens. In 2009, Governor Charlie Crist appointed Peter to the Florida Board of Education.

University Center Club Crab Cakes

1/2 cup mayonnaise

1 1/2 tablespoons Dijon mustard

1 1/2 extra-large eggs

1 tablespoon chopped cilantro

Juice of 1/2 lemon

3/4 tablespoon chopped garlic

1/2 teaspoon Tabasco sauce

1/4 teaspoon Worcestershire sauce

Salt and pepper to taste

1/2 loaf white bread, crust trimmed and bread cut into 1/2-inch cubes

1 1/2 pounds jumbo lump blue crab meat

1 tablespoon vegetable oil

Aïoli for topping

Minced fresh parsley to taste

Combine the mayonnaise, Dijon mustard, eggs, cilantro, lemon juice, garlic, Tabasco sauce, Worcestershire sauce, salt and pepper in a bowl and mix well. Fold in the bread. Let stand for 10 minutes. Fold in the crab meat, trying not to break up the lumps. Adjust the seasonings to taste. Shape into sixteen 3-ounce cakes.

Heat the oil in a nonstick sauté pan. Place the crab cakes carefully into the hot oil. Sear for 3 to 4 minutes on each side. Top with a dollop of aïoli and parsley.

CHEF TIM DROWN, UNIVERSITY CENTER CLUB

WINE PAIRING
Serve with a big, fat, creamy California chardonnay— citrus and tropical fruit that layer with hints of butter, anise, and tangy acidity.

TALLAHASSEE TIDBIT

Pulitzer Prize–winning author Mark Winegardner, a Florida State University English professor, was chosen to continue the "Godfather" novel series and has published two sequels about the Corleone family.

Crab Spaghetti

6 blue crabs
1/4 cup vegetable oil
1/4 cup extra-virgin olive oil
4 garlic cloves, chopped
1 (28-ounce) can whole plum
  tomatoes, chopped
1 tablespoon finely
  chopped parsley
Salt and pepper to taste
16 ounces spaghetti

Clean the crab by pulling off the top shells. Remove the gills with a scrub brush. Break the crabs into halves. Heat the vegetable oil in a large stockpot over medium heat. Add the crabs. Sauté for a few minutes until the crabs turn red. Remove the crabs and set aside.

Add the olive oil to the drippings in the stockpot. Add the garlic and sauté for a few minutes but do not brown. Add the tomatoes, parsley, salt and pepper and mix well. Add the crabs and simmer for 30 minutes.

Prepare the pasta in salted water using the package directions; drain. Remove the crabs from the sauce just before serving. Crack the crabs and pick the meat. Add the crab meat to the sauce and mix well. Toss the crab meat sauce with the hot pasta.

MICHAEL COLLEY

WINE PAIRING
Serve with Italy's version of Champagne, called Prosecco, which is great with crab and acidic tomato sauce. It is light and bubbly yet full enough to handle the sauce.

Budweiser-Braised Shrimp

MAKES 36

10 large garlic cloves, chopped
1/2 cup light olive oil
36 fresh shrimp, peeled
  and deveined
1/4 teaspoon cayenne pepper
Salt and black pepper to taste
12 ounces Budweiser beer
6 limes, cut into halves
6 ounces extra-dry vermouth

Cook the garlic in the olive oil in a large skillet over high heat for 2 to 3 minutes. Add the shrimp, cayenne pepper, salt and black pepper. Cook for 2 to 3 minutes. Add the beer and limes. Cook for 5 minutes or until the shrimp turn pink. Add the vermouth and serve.

TRIPP AND SUSIE BUSCH-TRANSOU FROM *Great Food Great Beer*, THE ANHEUSER-BUSCH COOKBOOK

WINE PAIRING
Serve with Spain's version of Champagne, called Cava. It is crisp and dry yet light and airy with touches of minerality. Segura Viudas is a favorite.

Grilled Scallops with Bacon Vinaigrette

SERVES 3 OR 4

4 slices bacon, chopped
1/2 cup vegetable oil
1/4 cup apple cider vinegar
1/4 cup sugar
2 teaspoons fresh lime juice
Salt and black pepper to taste
12 large sea scallops
1/2 cup vegetable oil
1/4 cup minced garlic
2 teaspoons kosher salt
2 teaspoons black pepper
2 teaspoons red pepper flakes

Preheat the grill to high. Fry the bacon in a large skillet over medium-high heat. Drain the bacon, leaving the bacon in the skillet. Add 1/2 cup oil, the vinegar, sugar and lime juice. Remove from the heat and sprinkle with salt and black pepper to taste. Keep warm. Toss the scallops with 1/2 cup oil, the garlic, 2 teaspoons kosher salt, 2 teaspoons black pepper and the red pepper flakes in a bowl. Thread the scallops onto metal skewers. Place on a grill rack. Grill for 3 to 4 minutes on each side or until opaque and slightly firm. Remove the scallops from the skewers and arrange on serving plates. Drizzle with the bacon vinaigrette and serve.

WINE PAIRING
Serve with a true French Champagne with plenty of finesse, airy texture, and mineral aromas.

Pot Roast Cabernet

SERVES 4 TO 6

2 to 3 tablespoons vegetable oil
3 to 4 pounds boneless beef
    chuck roast
4 to 6 tablespoons
    all-purpose flour
1 onion, studded with
    4 whole cloves
2 teaspoons salt
2 dried bay leaves
1 garlic clove, chopped
1 cup cabernet sauvignon
8 small onions, cut into quarters
8 carrots, cut into large sticks
1/2 head white cabbage,
    coarsely chopped

Preheat the oven to 350 degrees. Heat the oil in a large Dutch oven over medium heat. Coat the roast lightly with the flour. Brown gently on all sides in the hot oil. Add the clove-studded onion, salt, bay leaves and garlic. Add the wine. Bake, covered, for 2 hours. Remove from the oven. Add the small onions and carrots. Return to the oven and bake for 1 hour. Remove from the oven and add the cabbage. Return to the oven and bake for 30 minutes. Discard the clove-studded onion and bay leaves before serving.

WINE PAIRING
Serve with a French bordeaux such as mouiex merlot. It will have enough body yet not be over the top tannic or expensive.

Boursin Filets Mignons

SERVES 4

4 (8-ounce) filets mignons
1 teaspoon garlic salt
1 teaspoon pepper
2 teaspoons New Orleans-style
    seasoning such as Joe's Stuff,
    Victoria Taylor's or
    Prudhomme's
1 (12-ounce) bottle beer
5 ounces garlic and herb
    boursin cheese or Parmesan
    cheese, grated

Preheat the grill to 500 degrees. Place the filets in a deep pie plate or square baking dish. Rub 1/4 teaspoon garlic salt, 1/4 teaspoon pepper and 1/2 teaspoon New Orleans-style seasoning over each filet. Pour enough beer over the filets to fill the dish. Marinate for 10 minutes. Drain the filets, discarding the marinade. Place the filets on a grill rack and grill for 8 minutes. Turn the filets and grill for 6 minutes for medium-rare. Remove from the grill and immediately spread 1 to 2 teaspoons cheese over each filet. The cheese will melt over the surface of the filets. Serve immediately.

GREGG HOLGATE

WINE PAIRING
Serve with a rich, savory California cabernet sauvignon. Its leather, complex fruits, texture, and balanced herbaceous quality will pair well with this dish.

Goulash

2 beef bouillon cubes
2 cups hot water
3 cups chopped potatoes
2 cups water
1 pound sirloin, cut into
   1-inch pieces
1/2 Vidalia onion or other sweet
   onion, chopped
1 garlic clove, minced
Olive oil for sautéing
2 teaspoons Hungarian paprika
1 teaspoon salt
1/8 teaspoon pepper

Dissolve the bouillon cubes in 2 cups hot water in a bowl. Place the potatoes in 2 cups water. Sauté the beef, onion and garlic in olive oil in a 5-quart saucepan over medium heat until the beef is brown. Stir in the bouillon and undrained potatoes. Add the paprika, salt and pepper. Reduce the heat to medium-low. Cook for 4 hours, stirring occasionally.

EDITH PURPURA

WINE PAIRING
Serve with a delicious, intense, spicy shiraz or syrah with its black pepper tones and concentrated fruit.

Korean Barbecue Beef

1 pound London broil
2 tablespoons soy sauce
2 teaspoons sesame oil
4 scallions, finely chopped
2 garlic cloves, finely chopped
1 teaspoon finely chopped
   fresh ginger
2 tablespoons brown sugar
1 tablespoon rice vinegar
1/4 teaspoon pepper

Cut the beef into thin strips and tenderize. Mix the soy sauce, sesame oil, scallions, garlic, ginger, brown sugar, vinegar and pepper in a large bowl. Add the tenderized beef and mix well. Marinate in the refrigerator for 1 hour or longer to increase the flavor. Preheat the grill. Drain the beef, discarding the marinade. Place the beef on a grill rack. Grill over medium flame until cooked to the desired degree of doneness. The beef will cook quickly. Do not overcook.

MARY JAYNE SOKOLOW

WINE PAIRING
Serve with a spicy, jammy Australian shiraz with rich black fruits and layers upon layers of pepper.

Garden-Style Meat Loaf

2 eggs

2/3 cup milk

1 teaspoon salt

1/2 teaspoon freshly
　ground pepper

3 slices bread, crumbled

1 onion, chopped

1/2 cup shredded carrots

1 green bell pepper, chopped

1 cup (4 ounces) shredded cheese

2 pounds ground beef or
　ground turkey

1/2 cup ketchup

1/2 cup packed brown sugar

2 tablespoons yellow mustard

Combine the eggs, milk, salt, pepper and bread in a large bowl and mix well. Let stand until the bread absorbs the moisture. Add the onion, carrots, bell pepper, cheese and ground beef and mix well. Preheat the oven to 350 degrees.

Divide the meat mixture into two equal portions. Shape into loaves and place in two large loaf pans. Combine the ketchup, brown sugar and mustard in a small bowl and mix well. Pour over the loaves. Bake for 1 hour and 15 minutes or until cooked through. Remove from the oven and pour off any accumulated liquid. Let stand for 10 minutes before serving.

VERA PETERSEN

WINE PAIRING
Serve with a Napa Valley syrah with its concentrated fruit and mouth-coating tannins.

LIGHTEN UP

Meat loaf has been comfort food for generations. With the new options in lean ground beef today, this recipe can be adapted to fit into any healthy meal plan. Use extra-lean ground beef, eliminate or reduce the cheese, and substitute four egg whites for the two eggs. Short on time? Shape the ground beef mixture into "muffins" by filling muffin cups with individual servings. This bakes in about 25 minutes.

A THYME TO CELEBRATE

Taco Pizza

1 pound ground beef
1 envelope taco seasoning mix
1 pre-baked pizza crust
1 (16-ounce) can refried beans or
   fat-free refried beans
1 cup (4 ounces) shredded
   Cheddar cheese or
   mozzarella cheese
1 (16-ounce) jar taco sauce or
   picante sauce
1 (10-ounce) package
   shredded lettuce
Sour cream to taste
Sliced olives, optional

Preheat the oven to 450 degrees. Brown the ground beef in a large skillet, stirring until crumbly; drain. Stir in the taco seasoning mix. Prepare the pizza crust using the package directions. Spread the refried beans over the crust. Spread the ground beef mixture over the refried beans. Sprinkle with the cheese. Reduce the oven temperature to 425 degrees. Bake for 7 to 10 minutes or until the cheese melts. Remove from the oven and spread the taco sauce in an even layer over the top of the pizza. Sprinkle with the shredded lettuce. Cut into slices. Serve each slice with a dollop of sour cream and sprinkle with olives.

JOHN DAWSON, STAR 98 FM DJ

WINE PAIRING
Serve with Cline Ancient Vines red zinfandel. It is the perfect wine for this dish. It has flavors of dark berries and coffee, with great vanilla oak and lingering spicy black and white pepper.

Picadillo

1 (5-ounce) package yellow rice
1 tablespoon Worcestershire sauce
1 tablespoon extra-virgin olive oil
1 garlic clove, chopped
1/2 cup chopped red bell pepper
1 onion, chopped
1 potato, chopped
1/2 cup water
1 pound lean ground beef
1 teaspoon Adobo seasoning

Cook the rice using the package directions. Heat the Worcestershire sauce and olive oil in a large saucepan over medium-high heat. Add the garlic, bell pepper and onion. Cook for 5 to 10 minutes or until the vegetables are tender. Add the potato and water. Simmer for 3 minutes. Add the ground beef and Adobo seasoning. Cook, covered, until the ground beef is brown, stirring occasionally until crumbly. Cook until the potato is tender. Add additional Adobo seasoning or salt to taste. Serve over the rice.

ELLYN AIDMAN

WINE PAIRING
Serve with an Argentinean malbec with deep plum flavors and hints of licorice and tobacco.

Loranne Ausley's Lamb Kabobs

¹/2 cup red wine vinegar

¹/2 cup fresh lemon juice

2 tablespoons finely chopped
fresh parsley

1 teaspoon pepper

1 teaspoon ground cumin

¹/2 teaspoon salt

3 garlic cloves, minced

2 pounds leg of lamb, cut into
2-inch cubes

1 red bell pepper, cut into
8 pieces

1 yellow bell pepper, cut into
8 pieces

8 large mushrooms

1 eggplant, cut lengthwise
into quarters

1 zucchini, cut lengthwise
into halves

1 large Vidalia onion or other
sweet onion, cut into 8 wedges

Combine the vinegar, lemon juice, parsley, pepper, cumin, salt and garlic in a bowl and mix well. Place the lamb cubes in a sealable plastic bag. Add the marinade and seal the bag. Marinate in the refrigerator for 6 hours, turning the bag occasionally. Drain the lamb, discarding the marinade. Preheat the grill.

Thread the lamb cubes, bell peppers and mushrooms alternately on a set of eight metal skewers. Thread the eggplant, zucchini and onion alternately on another set of eight metal skewers. Place the vegetable kabobs on a grill rack. Grill over medium heat for 10 minutes on each side. Place the lamb kabobs on a grill rack. Grill over medium heat for 4 minutes on each side.

LORANNE AUSLEY AND BILL HOLLIMON

WINE PAIRING
Serve with a medium-bodied California pinot noir showing delicate and savory flavors of cedary oak and spicy black cherries.

TALLAHASSEE TIDBIT
Jim Morrison, lead singer for The Doors rock group, attended Florida State University in the early 1960s. During his time as a student at FSU, Morrison was arrested for a prank following a home football game.

Art Smith's Favorite Pulled Pork

SERVES 6 TO 8

1 1/2 pounds boneless pork butt
1/4 cup water
1 large white onion, chopped
1 jalapeño chile, seeded
  and chopped
2 tablespoons olive oil
2 tablespoons chili powder
1 1/2 teaspoons ground cumin
1 1/2 teaspoons coriander
1 1/2 teaspoons oregano
6 garlic cloves, minced
1/2 cup packed dark brown sugar
2 tablespoons molasses
1 (28-ounce) can crushed
  tomatoes
1 (16-ounce) can tomato paste
1 cup beef broth
1 bay leaf

Preheat the oven to 475 degrees. Place the pork on a wire rack in a Dutch oven. Add the water. Bake, uncovered, for 20 minutes. Cover and reduce the oven temperature to 300 degrees. Bake for 4 hours. Remove from the oven to cool. Pull the pork apart or shred and set aside.

Cook the onion and jalapeño chile in the olive oil in a Dutch oven just until tender. Add the chili powder, cumin, coriander and oregano and mix well. Add the garlic, brown sugar, molasses, undrained tomatoes, tomato paste, beef broth and bay leaf. Simmer for 20 minutes or until thickened. Discard the bay leaf. Add the pork to the sauce and mix well.

For variation, serve on Parmesan Goat Cheese Biscuits on page 77 or wrapped in flour tortillas with bread-and-butter pickles and sliced red onions.

CHEF ART SMITH

WINE PAIRING
Serve with a peppery, smoky red zinfandel with zesty tannins such as one from the Dry Creek Valley region of California.

Herbed Pork and Potatoes

SERVES 4 TO 6

1/4 cup olive oil
1 tablespoon minced fresh thyme, or 1 teaspoon dried thyme
2 teaspoons minced garlic
2 teaspoons dried minced onion
2 teaspoons minced fresh rosemary, or 1/2 teaspoon dried rosemary, crushed
1 teaspoon seasoned salt
1 teaspoon coarsely ground pepper
1 teaspoon ground mustard
2 dashes of Adobo seasoning
2 (1-pound) pork tenderloins
8 ounces small red potatoes, cut into quarters

Preheat the oven to 375 degrees. Combine the olive oil, thyme, garlic, onion, rosemary, seasoned salt, pepper, mustard and Adobo seasoning in a small bowl and mix well. Place the pork in a 1 1/2-quart or 9×11-inch baking dish. Drizzle the pork with three-fourths of the herb mixture. Toss the potatoes with the remaining herb mixture and arrange around the pork. Bake, uncovered, for 40 to 45 minutes or until the pork registers 160 degrees on a meat thermometer and the potatoes are tender. Let the pork stand for 5 minutes before slicing.

WINE PAIRING
Serve with an Oregon pinot noir that is ripe and gamey, showcasing pretty fruit and herbaceous earth layers.

Red Beans and Rice

SERVES 8 TO 10

1 package dried red kidney beans
Salt to taste
1 onion, coarsely chopped
1/2 cup chopped ham
2/3 cup Worcestershire sauce
3 bay leaves
6 garlic cloves, crushed
2 teaspoons dried basil
1 teaspoon Italian seasoning
1 tablespoon salt
1/2 package kielbasa, thinly sliced
5 dashes of Tabasco sauce
2 cups brown or white rice, cooked
Dash of Worcestershire sauce
Dash of Tabasco sauce

Soak the beans in salt water in a large bowl for 8 to 10 hours; drain. Place the beans in a slow cooker and cover with water. Add the onion, ham, 2/3 cup Worcestershire sauce, the bay leaves, garlic, basil, Italian seasoning, 1 tablespoon salt, the kielbasa and 5 dashes of Tabasco sauce and mix well. Cook, covered, on High for 4 hours, stirring occasionally. Reduce to Low and cook for 2 hours or until the beans are soft, stirring occasionally. Discard the bay leaves. Serve over the rice with a dash of Worcestershire sauce and Tabasco sauce.

NANCY CAIRE MILLER

WINE PAIRING
Serve with a Spanish garnacha (Grenache). Its kirsch, blackberry, and espresso tones are graceful yet edgy.

Sausage Meatballs and Gravy

2 tablespoons extra-virgin
  olive oil
12 garlic cloves, crushed
3 (14-ounce) cans diced tomatoes
1 (14-ounce) can tomato purée
1 (14-ounce) can tomato sauce
15 basil leaves, finely chopped
1 teaspoon nutmeg
1 tablespoon brown sugar
Salt to taste
1 package Italian bulk sausage
1 pound ground beef
3 eggs, beaten
1 1/2 cups (6 ounces) freshly grated
  Parmesan cheese
1 1/2 cups plain bread crumbs
1 teaspoon salt
1 teaspoon pepper
16 ounces linguini, cooked

Heat the olive oil in a medium stockpot over medium heat. Add the garlic and cook for 3 minutes, stirring constantly to prevent burning. Add the undrained diced tomatoes. Cook for 5 minutes. Add the tomato purée and tomato sauce. Cook for 5 minutes. Stir in the basil. Cook until the sauce bubbles. Reduce the heat by half. Add the nutmeg, brown sugar and salt to taste.

Combine the sausage, ground beef, eggs, cheese, bread crumbs, 1 teaspoon salt and the pepper in a large bowl and mix well. Shape into medium balls. Brown in a frying pan over medium heat. Add the meatballs to the gravy. Simmer for 1 hour and 30 minutes. Serve over the hot linguini.

JIM MAGILL

WINE PAIRING
Serve with a merlot. Layers of plum, spicy cedar, and roasted herb notes will do the job nicely.

TALLAHASSEE TIDBIT

The internationally renowned Boys' Choir of Tallahassee has played everywhere from the Kennedy Center to St. Peter's Basilica. In 2009, they performed during the inauguration celebration for Barack Obama. Director Earle Lee, Jr., won the Oprah's Angel Network "Use Your Life" award in 2002.

ENTRÉES

Roasted Chicken and Vegetables

SERVES 4

1 (3- to 4-pound) whole chicken
Olive oil for basting
Worcestershire sauce for basting
Garlic salt for sprinkling
Lemon pepper for sprinkling
2 sweet potatoes, peeled and cut
    into 1/4-inch pieces
1 onion, cut into 1/4-inch pieces
8 ounces grape tomatoes
8 ounces baby carrots
Hot cooked yellow rice

Preheat the oven to 350 degrees. Place the chicken breast side up in the center of a large roasting pan and baste with olive oil. Baste with Worcestershire sauce until coated. Sprinkle with garlic salt and lemon pepper to lightly coat.

Place the sweet potatoes, onion, tomatoes and carrots in a large bowl. Baste with the olive oil and Worcestershire sauce. Toss with your hands until the vegetables are coated. Sprinkle with garlic salt and lemon pepper to lightly coat and toss the vegetables again. Arrange the vegetables around the chicken. Bake until a meat thermometer inserted into the thickest portion of the chicken registers 165 degrees. Serve over hot cooked yellow rice.

CASSIE WILLIS CONN

WINE PAIRING
Serve with a dry, lean Italian pinot grigio with crispy citrus notes, stony mineral layers, and bracing acidity.

Oven-Baked Chicken Parmesan

SERVES 4

4 boneless skinless chicken
    breasts (about 1 1/4 pounds)
1 egg, lightly beaten
3/4 cup Italian dry bread crumbs
1 (26-ounce) jar marinara sauce,
    or 3 1/4 cups Tomato Sauce
    (page 72)
1 cup (4 ounces) shredded
    mozzarella cheese or Italian
    cheese blend

Preheat the oven to 400 degrees. Dip the chicken in the egg and then in the bread crumbs, coating well. Arrange in a greased 9×13-inch baking dish. Bake, uncovered, for 20 minutes. Pour the marinara sauce over the chicken. Sprinkle with the cheese. Bake for 10 minutes or until the chicken is cooked through. Serve over hot cooked pasta for a full meal, if desired.

WINE PAIRING
Serve with a Paso Robles merlot featuring youthful fruit with cherry, supple plums, and roasted sage tannins.

Pecan Chicken in Wine Sauce

14 boneless skinless
   chicken breasts
1¹/₂ teaspoons salt
¹/₂ cup plus 1 tablespoon
   all-purpose flour
3 cups sour cream
1¹/₂ teaspoons salt
3 (10-ounce) cans cream of
   mushroom soup, or 1¹/₂ cups
   Simple Cream of Mushroom
   Soup (page 48)
1¹/₂ cups dry white wine
1¹/₂ cups chopped pecans
¹/₂ cup chopped bell pepper
1 tablespoon paprika

Preheat the oven to 325 degrees. Place the chicken breasts side by side in two greased 9×13-inch baking dishes. Sprinkle with 1¹/₂ teaspoons salt. Combine the flour and one-half of the sour cream in a bowl and mix until smooth. Stir in the remaining sour cream, 1¹/₂ teaspoons salt, the soup and wine. Pour over the chicken. Sprinkle with the pecans, bell pepper and paprika. Bake for 1³/₄ hours or until the chicken is tender and cooked through.

WINE PAIRING
The obvious choice here is to use the wine you cooked with. Never cook with a wine you wouldn't drink. Try a dry, grassy sauvignon blanc with balanced acidity.

LIGHTEN UP
Perk up the nutritional profile of this dish in a flash with three changes that will make a significant dent in the fat and sodium content. Use fat-free or reduced-fat sour cream, reduce the amount of pecans, and choose healthier soup options to save on sodium and fat in this delightful entrée.

ENTRÉES

Polynesian Chicken

2 cups all-purpose flour
1 teaspoon salt
1/2 teaspoon pepper
4 to 6 chicken breasts
3 to 4 tablespoons vegetable oil
1 (20-ounce) can juice-pack
   sliced pineapple
1 (6-ounce) can pineapple juice
1 cup sugar
2 tablespoons cornstarch
3/4 cup cider vinegar
1 tablespoon soy sauce
1 chicken bouillon cube
1/4 teaspoon freshly ground ginger
1 green bell pepper, sliced
   into rings

Preheat the oven to 350 degrees. Mix the flour, salt and pepper in a large sealable plastic bag. Place the chicken in the bag and seal the bag. Shake gently until the chicken is thoroughly coated. Remove from the bag and shake off the excess flour.

Heat the oil in a large skillet over medium-high heat. Brown the chicken on each side and place in a single layer in a 9×13-inch baking dish.

Drain the pineapple, reserving the juice in a glass measure. Add enough of the pineapple juice to the reserved juice to measure 1 3/4 cups. Whisk the pineapple juice, sugar, cornstarch, vinegar, soy sauce, bouillon cube and ginger in a saucepan. Bring to a boil. Cook for 2 to 3 minutes or until slightly thickened, stirring constantly. Pour over the chicken. Bake, uncovered, for 45 minutes.

Place a slice of pineapple and a slice of bell pepper on each chicken breast. Bake for 20 minutes.

This recipe can be made with boneless skinless chicken breasts. Decrease the first baking time from 45 minutes to 20 minutes.

WINE PAIRING
Serve with a chardonnay showing ripe pineapple, juicy star fruit, and minimal oak, such as La Terre chardonnay from Sebastiani Vineyards.

Sweet Asian Chicken

SERVES 4 TO 6

1/4 cup wine or cooking sherry
1/4 cup vegetable oil
6 tablespoons brown sugar
1/4 cup soy sauce
1 garlic clove, minced
1/4 teaspoon dried oregano
4 to 6 boneless skinless
    chicken breasts
Hot cooked rice

Preheat the oven to 350 degrees. Mix the wine, oil, brown sugar, soy sauce, garlic and oregano in a bowl. Arrange the chicken in a single layer in a 9×12-inch baking dish. Pour the wine mixture over the chicken. Bake for 30 to 45 minutes, turning the chicken halfway through baking. Spoon the chicken and sauce over the rice.

BETSY CAIRE COUCH

WINE PAIRING
Serve with a spicy Australian shiraz to help counter the sweetness. It has flavors of rich blackberry fruit and spicy black pepper with layers of sweet oak.

Bruschetta-Stuffed Chicken Breasts

SERVES 4

1 (14-ounce) can Italian
    diced tomatoes
1 1/4 cups (5 ounces) shredded
    part-skim mozzarella cheese
1/2 teaspoon basil
1 (6-ounce) package stuffing mix
    for chicken
4 boneless skinless chicken breasts
1/3 cup roasted red pepper Italian
    Parmesan salad dressing

Preheat the oven to 350 degrees. Combine the undrained tomatoes, about 1/2 cup of the cheese, the basil and stuffing mix in a bowl and stir just until moistened. Place two chicken breasts in a large sealable freezer bag. Pound the chicken 1/4 inch thick with a meat mallet. Repeat with the remaining two chicken breasts. Place the chicken smooth side down on a cutting board. Spread each with one-fourth of the stuffing mixture. Roll up as tightly as possible, beginning at the narrow end. Place seam side down in a 9×13-inch baking dish. Pour the salad dressing evenly over the roll-ups. Bake for 35 minutes. Sprinkle with the remaining 3/4 cup cheese. Bake for 5 minutes longer or until the cheese melts and the chicken is cooked through.

AMY CLIBURN

WINE PAIRING
Serve with a dry Italian chianti (sangiovese) displaying blackberry, vanilla, and fine tannins.

Chicken Wellington Bundles

2 chicken breasts

8 ounces cream cheese, softened

1 bunch scallions, finely chopped

1 teaspoon salt

1/2 teaspoon pepper

2 (8-count) cans refrigerator crescent rolls or 2 refrigerator crescent dough sheets

2 (10-ounce) cans cream of chicken soup

3/4 cup skim milk

Dash of poppy seeds

Preheat the oven to 350 degrees. Place the chicken in a saucepan and cover with water. Bring to a boil over high heat and reduce the heat. Simmer for 20 minutes or until cooked through. Remove from the heat to cool. Shred the chicken, discarding the skin and bones. You should have around 3 cups shredded chicken. Beat the cream cheese, scallions, salt and pepper in a mixing bowl until creamy. Add the chicken and mix well.

Unroll the crescent roll dough and press the perforations to seal. Cut each sheet into four squares. Place a large spoonful of the chicken mixture on each square. Fold each square diagonally to enclose the filling and seal the edges. Make sure there are no rips, tears or openings. Place on an ungreased baking sheet. Bake for 30 to 35 minutes or until golden brown.

Bring the soup and milk to a simmer in a saucepan. Simmer, covered, for 15 minutes. Place the chicken bundles in a serving dish. Pour the soup over the bundles and sprinkle with poppy seeds. Serve immediately.

LAUREN SHOAF PATRICK

WINE PAIRING
Serve with a Russian River Valley sauvignon blanc displaying jalapeño chiles, grassy notes, and bracing acidity.

LIGHTEN UP

Quickly lighten this recipe with a few simple adjustments. Substitute healthier versions of ingredients found in your supermarket. Eliminate a portion of the fat and sodium by using the healthier cream of chicken soup, replacing the rolls with reduced-fat crescent rolls, and substituting reduced-fat cream cheese.

Summer Garden Chicken Pasta

2 pints grape tomatoes

8 ounces baby portobello
   mushrooms

2 tablespoons minced garlic

Salt and pepper to taste

1/2 cup plus 2 tablespoons
   olive oil

18 large basil leaves, julienned
   (1 ounce)

1/2 teaspoon crushed red
   pepper flakes

2 cups chopped cooked chicken

8 ounces angel hair pasta

Grated Parmesan cheese to taste

Preheat the oven to 400 degrees. Cut the tomatoes into halves and place in a shallow baking pan. Slice the mushrooms and add to the tomatoes. Sprinkle with the garlic, salt and pepper. Drizzle with 2 tablespoons of the olive oil. Toss gently to coat. Roast for 20 minutes or until the tomatoes are a bit shriveled.

Combine 1/2 cup olive oil, the basil and red pepper flakes in a large bowl and mix well. Add the chicken and roasted vegetables and toss well. Let stand until serving time.

Cook the pasta using the package directions. Drain well and return to the saucepan. Add the chicken mixture and toss well. Spoon into large individual serving bowls and sprinkle with cheese.

CASSIE WILLIS CONN

WINE PAIRING
Serve with Oregon pinot gris, which has more body than the Italian version, so it can handle the spice in this dish yet not be overpowered. It's lively with melon and soft green apple.

LIGHTEN UP
Fresh and flavorful, this pasta dish is cued up to be transformed into a fit and healthy favorite. The olive oil alone contributes a whopping 22 grams of fat and 200 calories per serving. Use nonstick cooking spray to roast the vegetables and reduce the olive oil by one-half. Boost flavor with a tablespoon or two of balsamic or your favorite flavored vinegar.

ENTRÉES

Peppy Chicken Burgers

SERVES 6

½ cup chopped red bell pepper
½ cup chopped orange
  bell pepper
Salt and pepper to taste
1 garlic clove, minced
1 pound ground chicken
1½ teaspoons Adobo seasoning
1 small egg, beaten
¼ cup plain bread crumbs
6 whole wheat buns

Preheat the grill. Sauté the bell peppers, salt and pepper in a small sauté pan over medium heat for 10 minutes. Add the garlic. Sauté for 2 minutes and set aside.

Combine the ground chicken and Adobo seasoning in a medium bowl and mix well. Add the egg, bread crumbs and bell pepper mixture and mix well. Rub your hands in additional bread crumbs and shape the mixture into six patties. The mixture will be very sticky. Place the patties on a grill rack. Grill until the patties are cooked through. Serve on the the wheat buns.

 WINE PAIRING
Serve with a spicy marsanne or roussanne delivering pure peach and apricot flavors with spicy white pepper notes.

Angel Chicken Pasta

SERVES 6

¼ cup (½ stick) butter
1 envelope Italian salad
  dressing mix
½ cup white wine
1 (10-ounce) can cream of
  mushroom soup, or 1 cup
  Simple Cream of Mushroom
  Soup (page 48)
4 ounces cream cheese
  with chives
6 boneless skinless chicken breasts
16 ounces angel hair pasta
Salt to taste

Preheat the oven to 325 degrees. Melt the butter in a large saucepan over low heat. Stir in the salad dressing mix. Add the wine and soup and mix well. Stir in the cream cheese. Heat until smooth, stirring constantly. Do not boil. Arrange the chicken breasts in a single layer in a 9×13-inch baking dish. Pour the sauce over the chicken. Bake for 1 hour.

Cook the pasta in boiling salted water in a large saucepan for 6 minutes or until al dente; drain. Cut the chicken into bite-size pieces. Serve the chicken and the sauce over the hot pasta.

 WINE PAIRING
Serve with a big, fat, buttery, oaky chardonnay. It would fit perfectly here. A ZD chardonnay from Napa would be outstanding.

Ratatouille Provençale

SERVES 6 TO 8

1 zucchini, peeled
1 eggplant, peeled
1 onion
4 tomatoes, peeled
1 green bell pepper
Olive oil for sautéing
Minced garlic to taste
Salt and pepper to taste
Chopped fresh basil to taste
Chopped fresh thyme to taste

Cut each vegetable into 1-inch pieces. Sauté each vegetable separately in olive oil, garlic, salt and pepper in a sauté pan just until tender. Combine the sautéed vegetables, basil and thyme in a bowl and toss to mix. Place in a large serving bowl and serve.

CHEF ERIC FAVIER, CHEZ PIERRE

 WINE PAIRING
Serve with a dry yet fruity French Côtes du Rhone, which is typically a blend of grenache, syrah, and mourvedre. It is fresh and lively, with snappy wild berry flavors shared by spicy, peppery notes.

Red Pepper Vodka Penne

SERVES 6

¹/₃ cup vodka
2 teaspoons red pepper flakes
1 onion, finely chopped
2 tablespoons butter
2 tablespoons olive oil
1 (28-ounce) can puréed or
    chopped tomatoes
1 cup heavy cream
Pinch of salt
16 ounces penne
1 (3-ounce) jar capers
Grated Parmesan cheese to taste

Mix the vodka and red pepper flakes in an airtight jar. Let stand for two days before using, shaking occasionally. Sauté the onion in the butter and olive oil in a large skillet until tender. Add the tomatoes. Cook over medium-high heat until almost all of the liquid has evaporated, stirring frequently. Stir in the cream and salt. Cook over medium-low heat. Strain the vodka mixture, discarding the solids. Add to the tomato mixture. Cook until thick and creamy.

Cook the pasta using the package directions. Drain well and return to the saucepan. Add the sauce and capers and mix gently. Serve immediately with cheese.

ORIGINALLY PUBLISHED IN *Finding Thyme*

 WINE PAIRING
Serve with Steele Shooting Star Black Bubbles. This is a sparkling shiraz that features creamy blackberry fruit but finishes very dry and crisp. Always a winner and very surprising.

ENTRÉES

{123}

Des·serts

[di·zurts]

1. Favorite part of any meal;

served first, if needed.

Pumpkin Cream Cheese Roll

MAKES 1 ROLL

3 eggs

2/3 cups canned pumpkin

1 cup granulated sugar

1 teaspoon baking soda

1/2 teaspoon cinnamon

3/4 cup all-purpose flour

2 tablespoons salted
   butter, softened

8 ounces cream cheese, softened

3/4 teaspoon vanilla extract

1 cup confectioners' sugar

Preheat the oven to 375 degrees. Grease a rimmed baking sheet. Line with waxed paper and grease the waxed paper. Beat the eggs, pumpkin, granulated sugar, baking soda, cinnamon and flour at medium speed in a mixing bowl until smooth. Pour into the prepared baking sheet. Bake for 10 to 12 minutes or until no batter remains on your fingertips when you touch the top lightly. Do not overbake. Invert onto a clean linen towel sprinkled with confectioners' sugar. Remove the waxed paper. Roll up in the towel and let cool completely.

Beat the butter, cream cheese and vanilla at low speed in a mixing bowl until creamy. Add 1 cup confectioners' sugar and beat until smooth. Unroll the cake from the towel. Spread the cake with the cream cheese mixture and roll up to enclose the filling. Wrap in plastic wrap and chill for up to two weeks or freeze for up to six months.

KATY HIGGINS RUDIE

Photograph for this recipe appears on page 124.

Chocolate Cherry Cake

SERVES 12

CAKE

1 (16-ounce) can cherry pie filling

2 eggs

1 teaspoon almond extract

1 (2-layer) package chocolate
   cake mix

CHOCOLATE GLAZE

1/4 cup sugar

1/4 cup water

1 cup (6 ounces) semisweet
   chocolate chips or dark
   chocolate chips

To prepare the cake, preheat the oven to 350 degrees. Combine the pie filling, eggs and almond extract in a bowl and mix well. Add the cake mix gradually, stirring constantly. Bake in two 8-inch cake pans using the package directions. Remove from the oven to cool.

To prepare the glaze, bring the sugar and water to a boil in a small saucepan. Remove from the heat. Stir in the chocolate chips immediately until smooth. Spread between the layers and over the top and side of the cake.

KITTY BALL

Flourless Chocolate Cake

CAKE

8 ounces good-quality semisweet
  or dark chocolate
1 cup (2 sticks) unsalted butter
1¼ cups sugar
1 cup good-quality baking cocoa
6 eggs
1 tablespoon vanilla extract
¼ cup cold decaffeinated coffee

CHOCOLATE GANACHE

2 cups heavy cream
18 ounces semisweet chocolate,
  chopped

To prepare the cake, melt the chocolate and butter in a double boiler, stirring frequently. Combine the sugar, baking cocoa and eggs in a mixing bowl and beat for 3 minutes or until frothy using the whip attachment on the mixer. Add half the chocolate mixture, beating constantly at low speed. Scrape down the side of the bowl after 1 minute using a rubber spatula. Add the remaining chocolate mixture and beat until smooth. Stir in the vanilla and coffee. Pour the batter into a sealable container and chill for several hours.

Arrange six 2×3-inch baking molds or six 8-ounce ramekins on a baking parchment-lined baking sheet. Chill in the refrigerator for 10 minutes. Preheat the oven to 325 degrees. Spray the baking molds with nonstick cooking spray. Pour the batter evenly into the baking molds, filling each two-thirds full. Bake for 20 to 25 minutes or until a wooden pick inserted in the centers comes out clean, the cakes are firm to the touch and the tops are slightly cracked. Let cool slightly.

To prepare the ganache, heat the cream in a saucepan until it begins to simmer. Place the chocolate in a heatproof bowl. Pour the cream over the chocolate and stir until smooth.

To assemble, unmold the warm cakes onto individual dessert plates. Spoon the warm ganache over the tops. Serve with ice cream or whipped cream and seasonal berries.

CHEF DAVID GWYNN, CYPRESS RESTAURANT

TALLAHASSEE TIDBIT
Florida State University's prestigious Flying High Circus was the first college student circus when it was founded in 1947, Florida State University's first year as a co-educational university.

Carrot Pineapple Cake

CAKE

1 cup vegetable oil
2 cups granulated sugar
3 jumbo eggs
2 teaspoons vanilla extract
2 1/2 cups all-purpose flour
1 teaspoon baking soda
1/2 teaspoon salt
2 teaspoons cinnamon
2 cups grated carrots
1 (2-ounce) jar baby food
   carrot purée
1 (8-ounce) can crushed juice-
   pack pineapple
1 1/2 cups chopped pecans
1 cup raisins (optional)

LEMON CREAM CHEESE FROSTING

8 ounces cream cheese, softened
1/4 cup (1/2 stick) unsalted
   butter, softened
2 teaspoons vanilla extract
8 ounces confectioners' sugar
2 teaspoons or more fresh
   lemon juice

To prepare the cake, preheat the oven to 350 degrees. Combine the oil, granulated sugar, eggs and vanilla in a bowl and mix well. Add the flour, baking soda, salt and cinnamon and mix until smooth. Stir in the carrots, carrot purée, pineapple, pecans and raisins and mix well. Pour into a greased 9×13-inch cake pan. Bake for 1 hour or until a wooden pick inserted in the center comes out clean. Let cool in the pan completely.

To prepare the frosting, beat the cream cheese, butter and vanilla in a mixing bowl until very smooth. Beat in the confectioners' sugar and lemon juice gradually at low speed until of a spreading consistency. Spread over the top of the cake in the pan. Cut into desired portions and serve.

SALLY KARIOTH

THYME SAVER

To get the most juice out of fresh lemons, limes, and oranges, roll them under your palm against the kitchen counter before squeezing. You also can microwave on High for 20 seconds before cutting and juicing them.

Double Decker Coconut Cake

CAKE

1 tablespoon cake flour
2 1/4 cups sifted cake flour
2 1/4 teaspoons baking powder
1/2 teaspoon salt
1 2/3 cups sugar
1/3 cup salted butter, softened
2 eggs
1 (14-ounce) can coconut milk
1 tablespoon vanilla extract

COCONUT FROSTING

4 egg whites, at room temperature
1/2 teaspoon cream of tartar
Dash of salt
1 cup sugar
1/4 tablespoon water
1/2 teaspoon vanilla extract
1/4 teaspoon coconut extract
2/3 cup sweetened flaked coconut

To prepare the cake, preheat the oven to 350 degrees. Coat two 9-inch cake pans with nonstick cooking spray. Dust with 1 tablespoon cake flour. Whisk 2 1/4 cups cake flour, the baking powder and salt in a bowl. Beat the sugar and butter at medium speed in a mixing bowl for 5 minutes or until light and fluffy. Add the eggs one at a time, beating well after each addition. Add the flour mixture and coconut milk alternately, beginning and ending with the flour mixture. Stir in the vanilla. Pour into the prepared cake pans and tap sharply on the countertop to remove any air bubbles. Bake for 30 minutes or until a wooden pick inserted in the centers comes out clean. Let cool in the pans on wire racks for 10 minutes. Invert onto wire racks to cool completely.

To prepare the frosting, beat the egg whites, cream of tartar and salt at high speed in a mixing bowl until stiff peaks form. Bring the sugar and water to a boil in a saucepan. Cook to 238 degrees on a candy thermometer, soft-ball stage; do not stir. Pour in a thin stream into the stiffly beaten egg whites, beating constantly at high speed. Stir in the vanilla and coconut extracts.

To assemble, place one cake layer on a cake plate. Spread with some of the frosting and top with 1/3 cup of the coconut. Top with the remaining cake layer. Frost the top and side of the cake with the remaining frosting. Sprinkle with the remaining coconut. Store, loosely covered, in the refrigerator.

KATY HIGGINS RUDIE

THYME SAVER

When separating eggs, break them into a funnel over a glass. The egg whites will fall through, leaving the yolk intact in the funnel. Egg whites should always be at room temperature before whipping. Be certain there is no yolk in the whites and that the bowl and beaters are perfectly clean. Cream, on the other hand, should be well-chilled. For the largest volume, chill the bowl and beaters before whipping.

Fizzy Bundt Cake

SERVES 10 TO 12

1½ cups (3 sticks) butter, softened
3 cups granulated sugar
5 eggs
3 cups all-purpose flour
2 tablespoons lemon extract
¾ cup lemon-lime soda
1 cup sifted confectioners' sugar
2 tablespoons fresh lemon juice

Preheat the oven to 350 degrees. Cream the butter and granulated sugar in a mixing bowl. Add the eggs and beat well. Add the flour 1 cup at a time, beating constantly until smooth. Beat in the lemon extract and lemon-lime soda. Pour into a greased and floured bundt pan. Bake for 1 hour and 15 minutes. Remove from the oven to cool completely. Invert onto a cake plate. Mix the confectioners' sugar and lemon juice in a small bowl until smooth. Drizzle over the cake.

JACKIE ATWELL

Muggle Cake

SERVES 1

¼ cup all-purpose flour
¼ cup sugar
2 tablespoons baking cocoa
1 egg, well beaten
3 tablespoons milk
3 tablespoons vegetable oil
3 tablespoons chocolate chips
  or nuts
Splash of vanilla extract

Mix the flour, sugar and baking cocoa in a microwave-safe coffee mug. Add the egg and mix well. Add the milk and oil and mix well. Stir in the chocolate chips and vanilla. Microwave on High for 3 minutes.

LILY ETEMADI

Chocolate Lover's Pound Cake

¹/₂ cup shortening

1 cup (2 sticks) butter, cut into
chunks and softened

3 cups sugar

5 eggs

3 cups all-purpose flour

¹/₂ cup baking cocoa

1 teaspoon baking powder

¹/₂ teaspoon salt

2 teaspoons vanilla extract

1 cup milk

Preheat the oven to 325 degrees. Beat the shortening and butter in a mixing bowl until creamy. Add the sugar and beat until light and fluffy. Add the eggs one at a time, beating well after each addition. Add the flour 1 cup at a time, beating until smooth after each addition. Stir in the baking cocoa, baking powder, salt and vanilla. Add the milk gradually, beating constantly until smooth.

Pour into a greased and lightly floured bundt pan. Bake for 1 hour and 20 minutes. Let cool in the pan for 3 to 5 minutes. Invert onto a cake plate to slice and serve warm or invert onto a wire rack to cool completely.

Serve with vanilla ice cream and fresh fruit such as strawberries. The cake can be made ahead of time and frozen. Remove from the freezer a day prior to serving to thaw.

BETTY SHATTUCK

THYME SAVER

Don't throw away your vanilla beans after you use them; there is still plenty of flavor left! Put those empty pods into an airtight container with granulated sugar. After a week or so, you'll end up with a delicately flavored sugar to use in your baking. Use the same technique with the zest of oranges, lemons, or limes for citrus sugar.

DESSERTS

Coconut Cream Cheese Pound Cake

3 cups cake flour, sifted
1/4 teaspoon baking soda
1/4 teaspoon salt
1/2 cup (1 stick) unsalted
    butter, softened
8 ounces cream cheese, softened
1/2 cup shortening
3 cups sugar
6 eggs, at room temperature
1 (6-ounce) package frozen
    coconut, thawed and
    at room temperature
1 teaspoon vanilla extract
1 teaspoon coconut extract

Preheat the oven to 325 degrees. Grease and flour a 10-inch tube pan and line with waxed paper. Sift the cake flour, baking soda and salt three times. Beat the butter, cream cheese and shortening in a mixing bowl for 2 minutes. Add the sugar gradually, beating constantly. Beat for 5 minutes longer, scraping the side of the bowl occasionally.

Add the eggs one at a time, beating only until the yellow disappears after each addition. Add the cake flour mixture one-third at a time, beating as little as possible after each addition. Stir in the coconut and flavorings. Pour into the prepared pan. Bake for 1 hour and 30 minutes. Let cool in the pan for 10 minutes before removing.

JEANNE CLARK FLOWERS

THYME SAVER
When a recipe calls for sifting, it works just as well to put all dry ingredients in the mixing bowl and stir with a whisk.

Rum Pound Cake

CAKE
1 cup chopped pecans
4 eggs
1 (2-layer) package yellow
  cake mix
1 (6-ounce) package instant
  vanilla pudding mix
1/2 cup cold water
1/2 cup vegetable oil
1/2 cup (80 proof) dark rum

RUM GLAZE
1/4 cup (1/2 stick) butter
1/4 cup water
1 cup sugar
1/2 cup dark rum

To prepare the cake, preheat the oven to 325 degrees. Grease and flour a 10-inch tube or bundt pan. Sprinkle the pecans in the bottom of the pan. Whisk the eggs in a large mixing bowl. Add the cake mix, pudding mix, water, oil and rum and mix well. Pour into the prepared pan. Bake for 1 hour. Let cool in the pan. Invert onto a cake plate. Prick the top of the cake with an ice pick.

To prepare the glaze, melt the butter in a saucepan. Stir in the water, sugar and rum. Boil for 5 minutes, stirring constantly. Remove from the heat. Drizzle evenly over the top and sides of the cake, allowing the cake to absorb the glaze.

THE LATE EVELYN SYKES

TALLAHASSEE TIDBIT

Goodwood Museum and Gardens was built in 1830 as the home of a cotton and corn plantation and now is listed in the National Register of Historic Places. Recognized for its architectural, economic, social, and political presence in the 19th century, the Italianate-style home reflects a style and sophistication rare in frontier Tallahassee and boasts more than 7,500 square feet.

DESSERTS

Sour Cream Pound Cake with Cream Cheese Icing

SERVES 10

CAKE
1 cup (2 sticks) butter, softened
1/2 cup shortening
3 cups sugar
6 eggs
3 cups all-purpose flour
1 teaspoon baking powder
1 cup whipping cream
1 teaspoon vanilla extract

CREAM CHEESE ICING
1/2 cup (1 stick) butter, softened
8 ounces cream cheese, softened
1 (1-pound) package
   confectioners' sugar
1 cup chopped pecans

To prepare the cake, preheat the oven to 325 degrees. Cream the butter and shortening in a mixing bowl. Add the sugar gradually, beating constantly until light and fluffy. Add the eggs one at a time, beating well after each addition. Add the flour, baking powder, cream and vanilla and mix well. Pour into a greased and floured tube pan. Bake for 1 hour or until the cake tests done. Let cool and invert onto a cake plate.

To prepare the icing, cream the butter in a mixing bowl. Add the cream cheese and beat until creamy. Add the confectioners' sugar and mix well. Stir in the pecans. Sifted all-purpose flour and whipping cream can be added to the icing for the desired consistency. Spread over the cake.

TALLAHASSEE TIDBIT
The oldest two continuously operating businesses in Tallahassee are Capital City Bank (founded 1895) and the Tallahassee Democrat *newspaper (1905).*

Raspberry Cheesecake

1 1/2 cups graham cracker crumbs
5 tablespoons butter, melted
3 tablespoons sugar
24 ounces cream cheese, softened
3 eggs, at room temperature
1 cup sugar
2 1/2 teaspoons vanilla extract
4 cups sour cream
6 tablespoons sugar
1 teaspoon vanilla extract
2 (10-ounce) packages
    frozen raspberries
2 tablespoons cornstarch
1/4 cup sugar

Preheat the oven to 350 degrees. Mix the graham cracker crumbs, butter and 3 tablespoons sugar in a bowl and mix well. Press in a 9-inch springform pan. Beat the cream cheese, eggs, 1 cup sugar and 2 1/2 teaspoons vanilla in a mixing bowl until smooth. Pour into the prepared pan. Bake for 35 minutes. Maintain the oven temperature. Chill for 30 minutes.

Combine the sour cream, 6 tablespoons sugar and 1 teaspoon vanilla in a bowl and mix well. Pour over the filling. Bake for 10 minutes. Chill for 4 hours or longer.

Combine the raspberries, cornstarch and 1/4 cup sugar in a saucepan. Cook over medium heat until thickened, stirring constantly. Remove from the heat to cool completely. Pour over the top of the cheesecake. Release the side of the pan and serve.

JANICE JORDAN TESCH

Chocolate Chip Dip

8 ounces cream cheese, softened
1/2 cup (1 stick) butter, softened
1/2 teaspoon vanilla extract
1/2 cup confectioners' sugar
2 tablespoons light brown sugar
1 (6-ounce) package miniature
    chocolate chips

Beat the cream cheese and butter in a bowl until fluffy. Add the vanilla, confectioners' sugar and brown sugar and beat until blended. Stir in the chocolate chips. Serve as a dip with graham cracker sticks or as a filling for cannoli shells.

KAREN JOINER

Pumpkin and Golden Raisin
Bread Pudding

SERVES 8

1 tablespoon unsalted butter
2 tablespoons canola oil
4 cups medium-diced
   local pumpkin
2 pinches of nutmeg
2 pinches of ginger
1 loaf dry multigrain bread,
   cut into 1-inch cubes
2 cups golden raisins
2 3/4 cups fat-free milk
2 eggs, lightly beaten
3 tablespoons Sugar in the Raw
2 tablespoons Tupelo honey
2 teaspoons vanilla extract
1 teaspoon cinnamon

Preheat the oven to 350 degrees. Melt 1 1/2 teaspoons of the butter over medium heat until frothy. Stir in 1 tablespoon of the canola oil. Add one-half of the pumpkin and sauté for 10 minutes or until evenly brown. Sprinkle with a pinch of nutmeg and a pinch of ginger. Spoon onto a plate. Repeat with the remaining butter, canola oil, pumpkin, nutmeg and ginger.

Arrange one-half of the bread evenly in a 9×9-inch baking dish sprayed with nonstick cooking spray. Layer one-half of the sautéed pumpkin and the remaining bread over the bread layer. Scatter with the raisins. Whisk the milk, eggs, 2 tablespoons of the sugar, the honey, vanilla and cinnamon in a large bowl. Pour over the layers. Cover with plastic wrap and let stand for 20 to 30 minutes or until the bread absorbs the liquid, frequently pressing down gently.

Remove the plastic wrap and arrange the remaining pumpkin over the top. Sprinkle with the remaining 1 tablespoon sugar. Bake for 45 to 55 minutes or until a wooden pick inserted in the center comes out clean. Let cool for 10 minutes before serving. Serve with vanilla frozen yogurt and confectioners' sugar.

CHEF BRIAN KNEPPER, THE GOVERNOR'S CLUB

Pumpkin Trifle

2 (14-ounce) packages pumpkin
   bread mix
1 (6-ounce) package vanilla
   pudding and pie filling mix
1 (30-ounce) can pumpkin
1/2 cup packed brown sugar
1/3 teaspoon cinnamon
1 cup brandy
12 ounces whipped topping, or
   Homemade Whipped Cream
   (page 145)
1/2 cup crushed gingersnaps

Prepare the bread mixes using the package directions and let stand until cool. Prepare the pudding and pie filling mix using the package directions and let stand until cool. Stir in the pumpkin, brown sugar and cinnamon.

Tear the bread into bite-size pieces. Layer the bread pieces, pudding mixture, brandy and whipped topping one-third at a time in a trifle bowl, packing down the layers. Sprinkle with the crushed gingersnaps. You also may add crushed gingersnaps between the layers, if desired. Chill, covered, for 8 to 10 hours before serving.

Kahlúa Trifle

1 (2-layer) package devil's food
   cake mix
1 (4-ounce) package instant
   chocolate pudding mix
3/4 cup Kahlúa
8 ounces whipped topping, or
   Homemade Whipped Cream
   (page 145)
1/2 cup chopped toffee crisp
   candy bars (about 4 bars)

Prepare the cake mix using the package directions and let stand until cool. Prepare the pudding mix using the package directions and chill in the refrigerator.

Tear the cake into bite-size pieces. Layer the cake, Kahlúa, pudding, whipped topping and candy bars one-third at a time in a trifle dish. Chill, covered, for 4 hours or longer before serving.

LAUREN SHOAF PATRICK

Chocolate Almond Torte

1 (23-ounce) package brownie
  mix with chocolate pieces
3 eggs
1/4 cup water
1 cup heavy whipping cream
1/4 cup sifted confectioners' sugar
1/4 teaspoon almond extract
1/4 cup baking cocoa
1 tablespoon water
2 teaspoons vegetable oil
2 teaspoons light corn syrup
2 cups sifted confectioners' sugar
1/2 cup sliced almonds, toasted

Preheat the oven to 350 degrees. Combine the brownie mix, eggs and water in a bowl and mix well. Pour into three greased and floured 8-inch cake pans. Bake for 12 minutes. Let cool in the pans on wire racks for 10 minutes. Remove to wire racks to cool completely. Beat the whipping cream at medium speed in a mixing bowl until foamy. Add 1/4 cup confectioners' sugar gradually, beating until firm peaks form. Stir in the almond extract. Spread between the torte layers.

Combine the baking cocoa, water, oil and corn syrup in a small saucepan. Cook over low heat for 2 minutes or until smooth, stirring constantly. Remove from the heat. Stir in 2 cups confectioners' sugar. Spread over the top and side of the torte. Arrange the almonds around the side, covering the spaces between the layers. Store in the refrigerator.

CAROLE STRANGE

Cream Puffs

1 cup water
1/2 cup (1 stick) unsalted butter
1 teaspoon granulated sugar
1 teaspoon salt
1 cup all-purpose flour
4 eggs
1 (4-ounce) package French
  vanilla instant pudding mix
1 cup heavy cream
3/4 cup milk
1/4 cup Irish Mist (optional)
Confectioners' sugar
  for sprinkling

Preheat the oven to 350 degrees. Bring the water, butter, granulated sugar and salt to a full boil in a medium saucepan over medium-low heat. Stir in the flour. Cook for 3 to 5 minutes or until the mixture forms a ball and leaves the side of the pan, stirring constantly with a wooden spoon. Remove from the heat and place in a food processor or a mixing bowl. Let cool for 5 to 10 minutes. Add the eggs one at a time, processing or beating constantly after each addition until the paste is smooth and shiny. Drop by spoonfuls onto a greased and floured large baking sheet. Bake for 50 to 60 minutes or until brown and firm. Let cool on a wire rack.

Beat the pudding mix, cream, milk and Irish Mist in a large mixing bowl for 2 minutes or until smooth and thick. Split the cream puffs and remove the doughy centers. Fill each with the pudding mixture. Sprinkle with confectioners' sugar.

STEPHANIE BRANDT AND PETER CORNAIS

Blueberry Yum-Yum

¹/4 cup cornstarch

3 tablespoons water

2 cups blueberries

1 cup sugar

¹/4 cup water

1 cup chopped pecans

¹/2 cup (1 stick) margarine

1 cup all-purpose flour

8 ounces cream cheese, softened

16 ounces whipped topping, or
  Homemade Whipped Cream
  (page 145)

Preheat the oven to 350 degrees. Dissolve the cornstarch in 3 tablespoons water in a small bowl. Combine the blueberries, sugar, ¹/4 cup water and the cornstarch mixture in a medium saucepan and mix well. Cook over medium heat until thickened, stirring constantly. Remove from the heat to cool.

Reserve some of the pecans for garnish. Cut the margarine into the flour in a bowl until crumbly. Stir in the remaining pecans. Press evenly in a 9×13-inch baking dish. Bake for 20 minutes. Remove from the oven to cool. Combine the cream cheese and one-half of the whipped topping in a bowl and mix well. Spread over the cooled crust. Spread the blueberry mixture over the cream cheese mixture. Spread the remaining whipped topping over the top and sprinkle with the reserved pecans.

TAMMY WEBB, STAR 98 MORNING SHOW CO-HOST

Berries on a Cloud

6 egg whites, at room temperature

¹/2 teaspoon cream of tartar

¹/4 teaspoon salt

1³/4 cups sugar

1 cup sour cream

1 cup sugar

1 teaspoon vanilla extract

1 cup whipped topping, or
  Homemade Whipped Cream
  (page 145)

8 ounces cream cheese, softened

1 pint fresh strawberries, sliced

Preheat the oven to 275 degrees. Beat the egg whites, cream of tartar and salt in a mixing bowl until foamy. Add 1³/4 cups sugar gradually, beating constantly at high speed until glossy and stiff peaks form. Grease the bottom and sides of a 9×13-inch glass baking dish. Spread the meringue evenly in the prepared dish. Bake for 1 hour. Turn off the oven. Let stand in the oven until cooled completely. Remove from the oven.

Beat the sour cream, 1 cup sugar, the vanilla, whipped topping and cream cheese in a mixing bowl until smooth. Spread on the baked meringue. Top with the strawberries.

JULIE KAY ROBERTS

Special Apple Pie

1 unbaked (9-inch) pie shell
1 cup sugar
1 tablespoon all-purpose flour
2 teaspoons cinnamon
Dash of salt
4 cups sliced peeled baking apples
1 egg, beaten
6 tablespoons butter, melted
1 teaspoon vanilla extract
1 cup chopped pecans

Preheat the oven to 400 degrees. Bake the pie shell using the package directions and set aside to cool. Maintain the oven temperature. Mix the sugar, flour, cinnamon and salt in a bowl. Add the apples and toss gently. Combine the egg, butter and vanilla in a bowl and mix well. Add to the apple mixture and mix well. Spoon into the prebaked pie shell. Sprinkle with the pecans. Bake for 10 minutes. Reduce the oven temperature to 350 degrees. Bake, loosely covered with foil, for 50 minutes longer.

ORIGINALLY PUBLISHED IN *Thymes Remembered*

Nutty Crust Cherry Pie

1 (11-ounce) package instant
   piecrust mix
1/2 cup slivered almonds,
   finely chopped
1 (21-ounce) can cherry pie filling
1 (14-ounce) can sweetened
   condensed milk
1/3 cup lemon juice
1 teaspoon vanilla extract
1/2 teaspoon almond extract
1/2 cup whipped topping, or
   1/2 cup Homemade Whipped
   Cream (page 145)

Preheat the oven to 450 degrees. Prepare the piecrust mix using the package directions, adding the almonds. Shape into a ball. Roll into a circle on a lightly floured surface. Fit into an 8-inch pie plate, trimming and fluting the edge. Prick the side of the pastry. Bake for 8 to 10 minutes or until golden brown. Remove from the oven to cool.

Heat the pie filling in a small saucepan over medium heat for a few minutes or until heated through, stirring occasionally. Remove from the heat to cool.

Mix the condensed milk, lemon juice, vanilla and almond extract in a bowl until the mixture thickens. Fold in the whipped topping. Spoon into the cooled pie shell. Top with the cooled cherry pie filling. Chill for 2 to 3 hours before serving.

CLIFTON QUINLY

Crunchy Cranberry Pie

SERVES 8

3 1/2 cups fresh or frozen
   cranberries
1/2 cup raisins
3/4 cup pecans, chopped
1/4 cup sugar
3 tablespoons all-purpose flour
1/4 cup light corn syrup
1 teaspoon grated orange zest
1 unbaked (9-inch) pie shell

Preheat the oven to 350 degrees. Pulse 1 3/4 cups of the cranberries and 1/4 cup of the raisins in a food processor six times or until coarsely chopped. Spoon into a large bowl. Repeat with the remaining cranberries and raisins. Add the pecans, sugar, flour, corn syrup and orange zest to the cranberry mixture and mix well. Spoon into the pie shell. Bake for 20 minutes. Cover the edges with foil and bake for 20 minutes longer. Remove from the oven to cool.

ORIGINALLY PUBLISHED IN *Finding Thyme*

Seven-Layer Squares

SERVES 16

1/2 cup (1 stick) butter
1 cup graham cracker crumbs
1 cup shredded coconut
1 1/2 cups (9 ounces) peanut
   butter chips
1 1/2 cups (9 ounces)
   chocolate chips
1 (14-ounce) can sweetened
   condensed milk
1 cup walnuts or pecans

Preheat the oven to 350 degrees. Melt the butter in a 9×12-inch baking pan and spread evenly. Layer the graham cracker crumbs, coconut, peanut butter chips and chocolate chips evenly in the prepared pan. Drizzle the condensed milk over the top, evenly covering the chips. Sprinkle with the walnuts. Bake, uncovered, for 30 minutes. Remove from the oven to cool. Cut into small squares.

KIM TABAH

Fudgy Amaretto Brownies

SERVES 15 TO 20

BROWNIES

1 1/4 cups (2 1/2 sticks) unsalted butter, melted

3/4 cup baking cocoa

4 eggs

2 cups sugar

2 teaspoons vanilla extract

1 teaspoon almond extract

1 cup all-purpose flour

1/4 teaspoon salt

1 1/2 cups chopped pecans

CHOCOLATE AMARETTO FROSTING

1/2 cup (1 stick) unsalted butter, softened

1/4 cup baking cocoa

1/4 cup amaretto

2 1/4 cups confectioners' sugar

To prepare the brownies, preheat the oven to 350 degrees. Combine the butter and baking cocoa in a bowl and mix well. Add the eggs and beat until fluffy. Add the sugar, vanilla and almond extract and mix well. Add the flour and salt and mix well. Stir in the pecans. Pour into a 9×13-inch baking pan. Bake for 30 minutes or until a wooden pick inserted in the center comes out clean. Remove from the oven to cool completely.

To prepare the frosting, beat the butter, baking cocoa, amaretto and confectioners' sugar in a bowl until smooth and creamy. If the frosting becomes too thick, add a teaspoon of water at a time until of the desired consistency. Spread over the cooled brownies.

TALLAHASSEE TIDBIT

The Springtime Tallahassee Festival was first held in 1968 to advertise the city's charms at a time when the Florida Legislature was threatening to move the state capital to a more central location. The first Tallahassee Winter Festival was held in 1987.

Sinful Brownies

4 ounces unsweetened
  baking chocolate
3/4 cup (1 1/2 sticks) butter
  or margarine
2 cups sugar
3 eggs
1 teaspoon vanilla extract
1 cup all-purpose flour
2 (6-ounce) bars Hershey's
  Symphony candy

Preheat the oven to 350 degrees. Place the baking chocolate and butter in a large microwave-safe bowl. Microwave on High for 2 minutes or until the butter melts, stirring at 30-second intervals until smooth. Stir in the sugar, eggs and vanilla. Add the flour and mix well. Spread in a greased and floured 9×13-inch baking pan. Press the candy bars into the batter. Bake for 30 to 35 minutes or until the brownies pull from the sides of the pan. Remove from the oven to cool. Cut into squares.

CHEF LINDA RICHARDS, THE CAKE SHOP

Very Best Blonde Brownies

2 3/4 cups all-purpose flour
2 1/2 teaspoons baking powder
1/2 teaspoon salt
3/4 cup (1 1/2 sticks)
  margarine, melted
1 (1-pound) package brown sugar
3 eggs, beaten
2 cups (12 ounces) semisweet
  chocolate chips
1 teaspoon vanilla extract

Preheat the oven to 350 degrees. Sift the flour, baking powder and salt together. Pour the margarine over the brown sugar in a large bowl and mix well. Stir in the eggs. Add the flour mixture and mix well. Stir in the chocolate chips and vanilla. Pour into a greased 9×13-inch baking pan. Bake for 30 minutes. Remove from the oven and let cool completely in the pan. Cut into bars.

ORIGINALLY PUBLISHED IN *Thymes Remembered*

Old-Fashioned Fudge

2 cups sugar
2 tablespoons light corn syrup
2 ounces semisweet chocolate
2 cups whipping cream
1/2 cup (1 stick) butter
1 teaspoon vanilla extract
1 cup chopped pecans

Bring the sugar, corn syrup, chocolate and whipping cream to a boil in a saucepan, stirring constantly. Cook to 234 to 240 degrees on a candy thermometer, soft-ball stage. Remove from the heat. Add the butter, vanilla and pecans and stir with a wooden spoon until the mixture loses its gloss. Pour into a buttered 9×9-inch pan. Let stand until completely cool. Cut into small squares.

THE LATE BEA HUFF

Nine-Minute Peanut Brittle

1 cup sugar
1/2 cup light corn syrup
1 cup dry roasted salted peanuts
1 teaspoon margarine
1 teaspoon vanilla extract
1 teaspoon baking soda

Mix the sugar and corn syrup in a 2-quart microwave-safe glass bowl. Microwave on High for 4 minutes. Stir in the peanuts. Microwave for 3 1/2 minutes. Stir in the margarine and vanilla. Microwave for 1 1/2 minutes. Remove from the microwave. Add the baking soda and stir until light and foamy. Pour in a thin layer on a lightly greased baking sheet. Let stand until cool. Break into pieces. Store in an airtight container.

CHERYL BOSENBERG MILES

Toffee Bars

48 salted saltine crackers
1 cup (2 sticks) butter
1 cup sugar
2 cups (12 ounces) milk
  chocolate chips or semisweet
  chocolate chips

Preheat the oven to 350 degrees. Line a baking sheet with foil. Arrange six rows of eight crackers on the prepared baking sheet. Bring the butter and sugar to a boil in a medium saucepan. Boil for 5 minutes. Spread over the crackers. Bake for 10 minutes. Remove from the oven. Pour the chocolate chips immediately over the top. Let stand until softened. Spread the chocolate evenly over the top. Let stand for a couple of hours or until cool. Break into pieces.

Homemade Whipped Cream

2 cups heavy whipping
  cream, chilled
1/4 cup confectioners' sugar
1 teaspoon vanilla extract

Whip the whipping cream in a mixing bowl with an electric hand mixer for 30 to 60 seconds or until it begins to thicken. Add the confectioners' sugar gradually, whipping until soft peaks form. Add the vanilla and beat until the peaks hold their shape. The entire process should take about 3 to 4 minutes or about twice as long if using a manual hand mixer or whisk. Do not overbeat. You may substitute other extracts, spices or liquors for the vanilla.

Cup·cakes, Coo·kies & Cock·tails

(kup'·kāks'), [koo·kees] &
(kŏk'·tals')

1. Perfect treats that incite happiness

and laughter.

Mandarin Orange Cupcakes

CUPCAKES

1 (2-layer) package yellow
   butter-recipe cake mix
4 eggs
1 1/2 cups vegetable oil
1 (11-ounce) can
   mandarin oranges

PINEAPPLE FROSTING

1 (20-ounce) can juice-pack
   crushed pineapple
1 (4-ounce) package vanilla
   instant pudding mix
12 ounces whipped topping, or
   Homemade Whipped Cream
   (page 145)

To prepare the cupcakes, preheat the oven to 350 degrees. Beat the cake mix, eggs, oil and mandarin oranges in a mixing bowl until blended. Pour into greased or paper-lined muffin cups. Bake for 20 to 25 minutes or until a wooden pick inserted in center of a cupcake comes out clean. Remove from the oven to cool.

To prepare the frosting, combine the undrained pineapple with the pudding mix in a bowl and mix well. Fold in the whipped topping. Spread over the cupcakes. Serve immediately or store in the refrigerator until serving time.

To prepare a three-layer cake, bake the batter in three well-greased 8- or 9-inch cake pans and let cool on wire racks. Spread the frosting between the layers and over the top and side of the cake.

PAM EDWARDS

Photograph for this recipe appears on page 146.

THYME SAVER
Transporting cupcakes is usually a challenge. Next time, place frosted cupcakes in a disposable muffin pan and invert a second disposable muffin pan on top as a cover. A piece of tape will keep them together, and your cupcakes will arrive in perfect condition.

Carrot Cupcakes with
White Chocolate Cream Cheese Icing   MAKES 12

CUPCAKES

1 1/2 cups all-purpose flour
1 1/4 teaspoons baking soda
1/2 teaspoon salt
1 1/2 teaspoons cinnamon
1/2 teaspoon nutmeg
1/4 teaspoon ginger
2 eggs, lightly beaten
1 cup plus 2 tablespoons
    granulated sugar
1/3 cup packed brown sugar
1/2 cup vegetable oil
1 teaspoon vanilla extract
2 cups shredded carrots
1/2 cup crushed pineapple
1/2 cup chopped pecans (optional)

WHITE CHOCOLATE
CREAM CHEESE ICING

2 ounces white chocolate
8 ounces cream cheese, softened
1/2 cup (1 stick) unsalted
    butter, softened
1 teaspoon vanilla extract
1/2 teaspoon orange extract
4 cups confectioners' sugar
2 tablespoons heavy cream
1/2 cup chopped pecans (optional)

To prepare the cupcakes, preheat the oven to 350 degrees. Mix the flour, baking soda, salt, cinnamon, nutmeg and ginger together. Beat the eggs, granulated sugar and brown sugar in a mixing bowl until light and fluffy. Add the oil and vanilla and mix well. Fold in the carrots and pineapple.

Add the flour mixture and mix until moistened. Fold in the pecans. Spoon into twelve lightly greased or paper-lined muffin cups. Bake for 25 minutes or until a wooden pick inserted in the center of a cupcake comes out clean. Let cool completely on wire racks.

To prepare the icing, melt the white chocolate in a small saucepan over low heat, stirring constantly until smooth. Remove from the heat and let cool to room temperature. Beat the cream cheese and butter in a mixing bowl until smooth. Add the white chocolate, vanilla and orange extract and mix well. Add the confectioners' sugar gradually, beating constantly until fluffy. Beat in the cream. Spread over the cupcakes and sprinkle with the pecans.

AMY CLIBURN

Cake Walk Cupcakes

MAKES 24

1 (2-layer) package yellow
  cake mix
3 eggs
1¼ cups milk
½ cup (1 stick) butter, melted
2 teaspoons almond extract or
  vanilla extract
2 teaspoons orange liqueur
  (optional)

Preheat the oven to 350 degrees. Line twenty-four muffin cups with paper liners. Combine the cake mix, eggs, milk, butter, almond extract and orange liqueur and mix well. Fill the prepared muffin cups three-fourths full. Bake for 20 minutes or until a wooden pick inserted into the center of a cupcake comes out clean. Let cool completely on wire racks before icing. See page 151 for icing suggestions.

ERICA VILLANUEVA

Chocolate Chip Cupcakes with Buttercream Frosting

MAKES 18

CUPCAKES
1 (2-layer) package white
  cake mix
¼ cup (½ stick) butter, softened
¼ cup packed light brown sugar
2 tablespoons granulated sugar
⅓ cup all-purpose flour
¼ cup confectioners' sugar
¼ cup miniature semisweet
  chocolate chips

BUTTERCREAM FROSTING
½ cup (1 stick) butter, softened
½ cup shortening
4½ cups confectioners' sugar
3 tablespoons milk
1½ teaspoons vanilla extract

To prepare the cupcakes, preheat the oven to 350 degrees. Prepare the cake mix using the package directions and set aside. Cream the butter, brown sugar and granulated sugar in a small mixing bowl. Add the flour and confectioners' sugar and beat until blended. Fold in the chocolate chips.

Fill paper-lined or greased muffin cups half full with the cake batter. Drop the chocolate chip mixture by tablespoonfuls into the center of each. Cover evenly with the remaining cake batter. Bake for 20 to 22 minutes or until a wooden pick inserted into the center of a cupcake comes out clean. Let cool in the muffin cups for 10 minutes. Remove to a wire rack to cool completely.

To prepare the frosting, cream the butter, shortening and confectioners' sugar in a large mixing bowl. Beat in the milk and vanilla until creamy. Spread over the cooled cupcakes.

Creamy Peanut Butter Icing

MAKES ENOUGH FOR
24 CUPCAKES

1 cup confectioners' sugar
1 cup creamy peanut butter
5 tablespoons unsalted
  butter, softened
3/4 teaspoon vanilla extract
1/4 teaspoon salt
1/3 cup heavy cream

Beat the confectioners' sugar, peanut butter, butter, vanilla and salt at medium-low speed in a mixing bowl until creamy, scraping down the side of the bowl with a spatula. Add the cream and beat at high speed until the mixture is light and smooth.

MARSHA MEDDERS

Pecan Coconut Frosting

MAKES ENOUGH FOR 24 CUPCAKES

1 cup sugar
1 cup evaporated milk
3 egg yolks
1/2 cup (1 stick) unsalted butter,
  cut into small cubes
1/2 teaspoon vanilla extract
1 1/3 cups sweetened
  flaked coconut
1 1/3 cups chopped pecans

Combine the sugar, evaporated milk, egg yolks, butter and vanilla in a saucepan and mix well. Cook over medium heat until thickened, stirring constantly. Remove from the heat. Stir in the coconut and pecans. Continue stirring or mixing with an electric mixer until cool and thick. Let cool completely before using.

Cream Cheese Frosting

MAKES ENOUGH FOR 24 CUPCAKES

8 ounces cream cheese, softened
1/4 cup (1/2 stick) unsalted
  butter, softened
2 cups confectioners' sugar
2 teaspoons vanilla extract
1/2 teaspoon fresh lemon juice

Beat the cream cheese and butter in a mixing bowl until fluffy. Beat in the confectioners' sugar gradually until smooth. Stir in the vanilla and lemon juice.

CUPCAKES, COOKIES & COCKTAILS

Chocolate Cheesecake Cupcakes

1 (2-layer) package chocolate
  cake mix
8 ounces cream cheese, softened
1 egg
1/3 cup sugar
6 ounces miniature semisweet
  chocolate chips

Preheat the oven using the cake mix package directions. Line twenty-four muffin cups with paper liners. Prepare the cake mix using the package directions. Beat the cream cheese, egg and sugar in a mixing bowl until smooth. Fold in the chocolate chips.

Fill each paper-lined muffin cup two-thirds full with the chocolate batter. Swirl a spoonful of the cream cheese mixture on top of the batter. Bake using the package directions. Do not let the cream cheese mixture brown.

HALLEY STINCHFIELD

Lemonade Cupcakes

1 (6-ounce) can frozen lemonade
  concentrate, thawed
1 (2-layer) package white
  cake mix
1 cup sour cream
3 ounces cream cheese, softened
3 eggs
Cream Cheese Frosting (page 151)

Preheat the oven to 350 degrees. Remove 2 tablespoons of the lemonade concentrate and reserve for another use. Beat the remaining lemonade concentrate, the cake mix, sour cream, cream cheese and eggs at low speed in a mixing bowl until moistened. Beat at high speed for 3 minutes, stopping occasionally to scrape down the side. Spoon into thirty paper-lined muffin cups, filling each three-fourths full. Bake for 20 to 25 minutes or until a wooden pick inserted in the center of a cupcake comes out clean. Remove the cupcakes from the pan and cool completely on a wire rack. Spread evenly with the frosting.

Monster Pistachio Pecan Cupcakes

CUPCAKES

1 (2-layer) package yellow
  cake mix
2 (4-ounce) packages pistachio
  instant pudding mix
4 eggs
3/4 cup water
2/3 cup vegetable oil
1/3 cup sugar
1/2 teaspoon cinnamon
1/4 cup chopped pecans

CINNAMON PECAN GLAZE

1/4 cup (1/2 stick) butter, melted
2 1/2 cups confectioners' sugar
3 tablespoons hot water
1 teaspoon vanilla extract
1/2 teaspoon cinnamon
1/2 cup chopped pecans

To prepare the cupcakes, preheat the oven to 350 degrees. Combine the cake mix, pudding mix, eggs, water and oil in a large mixing bowl and beat for 7 minutes, beginning at medium speed and increasing to high speed. Mix the sugar, cinnamon and pecans in a small bowl.

Layer some of the cake batter, 1 teaspoon of the pecan mixture and some remaining cake batter in each paper-lined muffin cup. Bake for 15 to 18 minutes or until the cupcakes test done. Do not overbake. Remove to wire racks to cool.

To prepare the glaze, combine the butter, confectioners' sugar, hot water, vanilla, cinnamon and pecans in a small mixing bowl and mix well. Spread a thin layer of the glaze over the cooled cupcakes.

JENNIFER WOMBLE

TALLAHASSEE TIDBIT

Frenchman Prince Achille Murat, nephew of Napoleon Bonaparte, had a plantation in neighboring Jefferson County. In 1826 he married George Washington's great-grandniece, Catherine Dangerfield Willis Gray, in Tallahassee. Princess Murat's home, Bellevue, is on permanent display at the Tallahassee Museum of History and Natural Science.

Red Velvet Cupcakes

CUPCAKES

2¹/₂ cups all-purpose flour

1 teaspoon baking soda

2¹/₂ tablespoons baking cocoa

1¹/₂ cups vegetable oil

1¹/₂ cups sugar

2 eggs

1 cup buttermilk

1 teaspoon white vinegar

1 (1-ounce) bottle red food
    coloring

2 teaspoons vanilla extract

NUTTY CREAM CHEESE FROSTING

1 cup (2 sticks) butter, softened

8 ounces cream cheese, softened

1 teaspoon vanilla extract

1 (1-pound) package
    confectioners' sugar

1 cup pecans

To prepare the cupcakes, preheat the oven to 325 degrees. Lightly oil and flour twenty-four muffin cups or line with paper liners. Sift the flour, baking soda and baking cocoa together. Combine the oil, sugar, eggs, buttermilk and vinegar in a mixing bowl and mix well. Stir in the flour mixture. Add the food coloring and vanilla and mix well. Spoon into the prepared muffin cups. Bake for 25 to 30 minutes or until the cupcakes test done. Remove to wire racks to cool completely.

To prepare the frosting, cream the butter and cream cheese in a mixing bowl. Add the vanilla and beat well. Add the confectioners' sugar gradually, beating constantly until smooth. Stir in the pecans. Spread over the cupcakes.

MARSHA MEDDERS

THYME SAVER

If you are ever in need of a buttermilk substitute, use this formula: To 1 cup of warm milk add either 1¹/2 tablespoons fresh lemon juice or 1¹/3 tablespoons cider vinegar. Allow this mixture to stand for 5 to 10 minutes. This works in a pinch but nothing beats the real thing.

Pineapple Rum Cupcakes

2 1/4 cups all-purpose flour
1 teaspoon baking soda
1 teaspoon salt
1 1/2 cups (3 sticks) butter
3 cups sugar
4 eggs
2 cups finely chopped pineapple
1/2 cup pineapple juice
3 tablespoons rum
1 cup pecans, finely chopped
Homemade Whipped Cream
   (page 145)

Preheat the oven to 350 degrees. Mix the flour, baking soda and salt together. Place the butter in a large microwave-safe glass bowl. Microwave on High at 30-second intervals until melted. Add the sugar gradually, beating constantly. Add the eggs, pineapple, pineapple juice and rum and mix well. Beat in the flour mixture gradually. Fold in the pecans. Fill paper-lined muffin cups to the top. Bake for 25 minutes or until set. Remove from the oven to cool completely. Frost with Homemade Whipped Cream.

Almond Cookies

1 cup (2 sticks) butter, softened
3/4 cup granulated sugar
3/4 teaspoon almond extract
2 cups all-purpose flour
1/2 teaspoon baking powder
1/4 teaspoon salt
1 cup confectioners' sugar
1 teaspoon almond extract
2 to 3 teaspoons water
1/2 cup sliced almonds

Preheat the oven to 400 degrees. Combine the butter, granulated sugar and 3/4 teaspoon almond extract in a large mixing bowl. Beat at medium speed for 1 to 2 minutes or until creamy, scraping the side of the bowl frequently. Reduce the speed to low and add the flour, baking powder and salt. Beat for 1 to 2 minutes or until mixed.

Shape the dough into 1-inch balls. Place 2 inches apart on a nonstick cookie sheet. Flatten each ball to 1/4 inch with the bottom of a buttered glass dipped in sugar. Bake for 7 to 9 minutes or until the edges are light brown. Let cool on the cookie sheet for 1 minute. Remove to a wire rack to cool completely. Whisk the confectioners' sugar, 1 teaspoon almond extract and water in a small mixing bowl. Spread over the cool cookies and top with sliced almonds.

JANICE JORDAN TESCH

Blizzard Cookies

2 cups quick-cooking oats

2 cups Special K cereal

4 cups all-purpose flour

2 teaspoons baking soda

2 teaspoons baking powder

2 cups (4 sticks) unsalted
  butter, melted

2 cups packed brown sugar

2 cups granulated sugar

2 teaspoons vanilla extract

4 eggs

1 1/2 cups raisins

1 cup sweetened flaked coconut

1 cup chopped pecans

Preheat the oven to 350 degrees. Process the oats and cereal in a blender or food processor to a fine powder. Mix the flour, baking soda and baking powder together. Beat the butter, brown sugar, granulated sugar and vanilla in an extra-large mixing bowl. Add the eggs one at a time, beating well after each addition.

Add the oat mixture, raisins, coconut and pecans, mixing well after each addition. Add the flour mixture and mix well. The dough will be very stiff. Drop the dough by spoonfuls onto a nonstick cookie sheet. Bake for 10 minutes or until golden brown. Let cool on a wire rack.

AMANDA KARIOTH THOMPSON

TALLAHASSEE TIDBIT

There have been seven measurable snowfalls in Tallahassee. The most recent was December 22–23, 1989 (1.0 inch). The biggest snowfall was February 12–13, 1958, when 2.8 inches fell.

Chocolate Cake Cookies

MAKES 4 DOZEN

1 (2-layer) package devil's food
   cake mix
2 eggs, beaten
1/2 cup vegetable oil
1 teaspoon vanilla extract
2 cups (12 ounces) semisweet
   chocolate chips

Preheat the oven to 350 degrees. Combine the cake mix, eggs, oil and vanilla in a mixing bowl and mix well. Stir in the chocolate chips. Drop by spoonfuls onto an ungreased cookie sheet. Bake for 8 to 10 minutes or until firm. Let cool on the cookie sheet for 5 minutes. Remove to a wire rack to cool completely.

SARAH MAXWELL

Chocolate Chip Pumpkin Cookies MAKES 8 1/2 DOZEN

4 cups all-purpose flour
2 cups quick-cooking oats
2 teaspoons baking soda
2 teaspoons cinnamon
1 teaspoon salt
1 1/2 cups (3 sticks)
   butter, softened
2 cups packed brown sugar
1 cup granulated sugar
1 (15-ounce) can pumpkin
1 egg
1 teaspoon vanilla extract
2 cups (12 ounces) semisweet
   chocolate chips

Preheat the oven to 350 degrees. Mix the flour, oats, baking soda, cinnamon and salt together. Cream the butter, brown sugar and granulated sugar in a large mixing bowl. Add the pumpkin, egg and vanilla and mix well. Add the flour mixture gradually, mixing well after each addition. Stir in the chocolate chips. Drop by tablespoonfuls 2 inches apart onto an ungreased cookie sheet. Bake for 10 to 12 minutes or until light brown. Let cool completely on a wire rack.

JILLIAN HOOVER

Peanut Butter Cookies

$^1/_2$ cup (1 stick) butter, softened
$^1/_2$ cup granulated sugar
$^1/_2$ cup packed brown sugar
1 egg
1 teaspoon vanilla extract
1 cup creamy peanut butter
1$^1/_2$ cups unbleached flour
$^1/_2$ teaspoon baking soda
1 cup (6 ounces) milk
  chocolate chips
1 cup (6 ounces) peanut
  butter chips

Preheat the oven to 350 degrees. Cream the butter, granulated sugar and brown sugar in a mixing bowl. Add the egg and vanilla and mix well. Add the peanut butter and mix well. Add the flour and baking soda gradually, beating constantly. Stir in the milk chocolate chips and peanut butter chips. Drop by small ice cream scoopfuls onto a nonstick cookie sheet. Bake for 9 minutes or until golden brown. Let cool on a wire rack.

CHEF LINDA RICHARDS, THE CAKE SHOP

Festive Cream Cheese Cookies

2$^1/_2$ cups all-purpose flour
$^1/_2$ teaspoon salt
1 cup (2 sticks) butter or
  margarine, softened
8 ounces cream cheese, softened
1 cup granulated sugar
$^1/_2$ teaspoon vanilla extract
$^1/_2$ cup finely chopped pecans
Red and green sugar crystals
  for coating

Mix the flour and salt together. Cream the butter and cream cheese in a large mixing bowl. Add the granulated sugar and vanilla and beat until light and fluffy. Add the flour mixture gradually, beating constantly until blended. Stir in the pecans. Divide the dough into four equal portions. Shape each portion into a 6-inch roll 1$^1/_2$ inches in diameter. Place each in the center of four sheets of heavy-duty foil. Bring two sides of the foil up over each roll. Fold down in locked folds until the foil is tight against the roll. Fold the short ends up and over and crimp to seal. Chill overnight or freeze.

Preheat the oven to 325 degrees. Remove the rolls from the refrigerator or freezer. Unwrap and coat each roll with sugar crystals. Cut into $^1/_4$-inch slices. Place on an ungreased cookie sheet. Bake for 15 to 18 minutes or until the bottom of each cookie is light brown when lifted. Remove to a wire rack to cool.

Pecan Crescent Cookies

1 cup (2 sticks) unsalted
  butter, softened
1/2 cup granulated sugar
2 cups all-purpose flour
1 tablespoon water
2 cups finely chopped pecans
1 teaspoon vanilla extract
Confectioners' sugar for rolling
Granulated sugar for rolling

Preheat the oven to 300 degrees. Cream the butter in a mixing bowl. Add 1/2 cup granulated sugar and beat until light and fluffy. Add the flour, water, pecans and vanilla and mix well. Roll the dough into tablespoon-size balls and then shape into crescent shapes. Roll in confectioners' sugar and place on a nonstick cookie sheet. Bake for 35 minutes. Let cool completely on a wire rack. Roll in granulated sugar.

Melting Moments

1 cup (2 sticks) butter, softened
1/3 cup confectioners' sugar
1 cup all-purpose flour
3/4 cup cornstarch
3 ounces cream cheese, softened
1 cup confectioners' sugar
1 teaspoon vanilla extract
Few drops of food coloring

Preheat the oven to 350 degrees. Cream the butter and 1/3 cup confectioners' sugar in a mixing bowl. Add the flour and cornstarch and mix well. Cover and chill the dough. Shape into 1-inch balls and place on an ungreased cookie sheet. Make an indentation with your thumb in the middle of each ball. Bake for 10 to 12 minutes or until brown. Remove from the cookie sheet to cool.

Beat the cream cheese and 1 cup confectioners' sugar in a mixing bowl until smooth. Add the vanilla and food coloring and mix well. Place a spoonful in the indention of each cookie.

ORIGINALLY PUBLISHED IN *Thymes Remembered*

Anise Almond Biscotti

3¼ cups all-purpose flour
1 tablespoon baking powder
⅓ teaspoon salt
1½ cups sugar
½ cup plus 2 tablespoons
  unsalted butter, melted
3 eggs
1 tablespoon vanilla extract
2 teaspoons anise seeds, toasted
  and bruised
1 cup whole almonds, toasted
  and coarsely chopped

Preheat the oven to 350 degrees. Sift the flour, baking powder and salt into a medium bowl. Mix the sugar, butter, eggs, vanilla and anise seeds in a large bowl. Add the flour mixture and stir with a spoon until blended. Stir in the almonds.

Divide the dough into two equal portions. Shape each portion into logs 13½ inches long by 2½ inches wide. Place several inches apart on a baking sheet lined with parchment paper. Bake for 30 minutes or until golden brown. The logs will spread. Remove to a wire rack to cool for 25 minutes. Maintain the oven temperature.

Place the logs on a cutting board. Cut the logs diagonally into ½-inch slices. Place on a baking sheet. Bake for 10 minutes. Turn and bake for 5 minutes longer. Let cool on a wire rack. For variation, add 1 cup miniature chocolate chips to the batter, or dip the biscotti into melted chocolate.

CATHY BISHOP

TALLAHASSEE TIDBIT

Tallahassee touts six "official" canopy roads—Miccosukee, Centerville, Old St. Augustine, Old Centerville, Meridian, and Old Bainbridge—that create emerald tunnels of ancient moss-draped live oaks and are listed among the "Top 10 Scenic Byways in America." The roads came into existence from old Indian trails which then became market roads that plantation owners lined with live oaks. Light filters down through them by day, then becoming mysterious tunnels of darkness on moonless nights.

A THYME TO CELEBRATE

Funky Rum Drink

SERVES 6

2 1/2 cups cranberry juice cocktail
3 cups orange juice
1 cup orange rum

Combine the cranberry juice cocktail, orange juice and rum in a pitcher and blend well. Pour into ice-filled glasses.

ORIGINALLY PUBLISHED IN *Finding Thyme*

Minty Lemon Ice

SERVES 16

1 pint vodka
1 (12-ounce) can frozen
   lemonade concentrate, thawed
2 liters lemon-lime soda
Mint leaves for garnish

Combine the vodka, lemonade concentrate and lemon-lime soda in a bowl and blend well. Pour into a 4-quart freezer container. Freeze for 8 to 10 hours. Thaw for 2 to 3 hours or until slushy before serving. Pour into highball glasses and garnish with mint leaves. Any unused portion may be refrozen for up to a month.

ORIGINALLY PUBLISHED IN *Finding Thyme*

Red Apple Sangria

SERVES 16 TO 20

1 1/2 bottles merlot, chilled
6 to 8 ounces red apple liqueur,
   or to taste, chilled
4 ounces grenadine, or
   to taste, chilled
32 ounces cranberry juice
   cocktail, chilled
32 ounces pineapple
   juice, chilled
2 liters lemon-lime soda, chilled
Fresh cherries, apple slices, lime
   wedges and orange wedges
   for garnish

Combine the merlot, apple liqueur, grenadine, cranberry juice cocktail, pineapple juice and lemon-lime soda in a large pitcher and blend well. Add cherries, apple slices, lime wedges and orange wedges for garnish. Pour into highball glasses or wine glasses.

Orange Devil

1 1/4 cups sugar
1 1/4 cups water
1 1/4 cups fresh lime juice
   (about 8 limes)
3 pounds oranges, peeled
   and chopped
2 1/4 cups good-quality
   orange-flavored vodka
1 (750-milliliter) bottle
   sparkling water
Orange slices or strawberries
   for garnish

Bring the sugar and water to a boil in a small saucepan, stirring constantly until the sugar is dissolved. Remove from the heat to cool. Mix the lime juice and one-half of the oranges in a large glass bowl. Stir in the sugar syrup. Add the remaining oranges. Purée with an immersion blender or in a blender. Chill, covered, for 1 to 10 hours.

Stir in the vodka. Fill twelve glasses with ice. Spoon 1/2 cup of the orange mixture into each glass. Top with the sparkling water and serve immediately. Garnish with orange slices or strawberries.

Southern Old-Fashioned

2 to 4 parts high-quality bourbon
2 parts lemon-lime soda
1 part club soda
Splash of cherry juice
Juice of 1/2 orange
Dash of angostura bitters
Cherries and orange slices
   for garnish

Combine the bourbon, lemon-lime soda, club soda, cherry juice, orange juice and angostura bitters in a large shaker and shake gently. Pour over crushed ice in an old-fashioned glass. Garnish with cherries and orange slices.

DR. STEPHEN F. X. ZIEMAN

Tickled Pink

1 (12-ounce) bottle
 lemon-flavored beer
1 (12-ounce) can frozen pink
 lemonade concentrate, thawed
1 cup vodka
Crushed ice
4 lime wedges

Mix the beer, lemonade concentrate and vodka in a bowl. Fill a blender container halfway with crushed ice and add one-half of the beer mixture. Process until slushy. Pour into a serving pitcher. Repeat with the remaining beer mixture and crushed ice. Pour into glasses and garnish each with a lime wedge.

ORIGINALLY PUBLISHED IN *Finding Thyme*

Champagne Holiday Punch

1 (64-ounce) bottle cranberry
 juice cocktail, chilled
1 cup sugar
1 bottle rosé, chilled
1 bottle Champagne
Mint leaves for garnish

Combine the cranberry juice cocktail and sugar in a pitcher and stir until dissolved. Chill for at least 1 hour or until serving time. Combine with the wine and Champagne in a large punch bowl. Ladle into punch cups or serve in fluted Champagne glasses. Garnish with mint leaves.

ORIGINALLY PUBLISHED IN *Thymes Remembered*

CUPCAKES, COOKIES & COCKTAILS

Cran-Strawberry Champagne Punch

SERVES 14

1 (10-ounce) package frozen
   strawberries, thawed
1/2 cup sugar
1/2 cup brandy
1 (48-ounce) bottle cranberry
   juice cocktail, chilled
1 (750-milliliter) bottle
   Champagne, chilled
1 (28-ounce) bottle club
   soda, chilled

Mash the strawberries with a fork in a large bowl. Stir in the sugar, brandy and cranberry juice cocktail. Freeze, covered, until firm. Place in a punch bowl about 2 hours before serving. Add the Champagne and club soda. Ladle into punch cups.

Holiday Cranberry Punch

SERVES 20

2 cups orange juice
1/3 cup lemon juice
1/2 cup sugar
1 (48-ounce) bottle cranberry
   juice cocktail
2 pints raspberry sherbet
2 (28-ounce) bottles
   ginger ale, chilled

Combine the orange juice, lemon juice and sugar in a pitcher and stir until the sugar dissolves. Add the cranberry juice cocktail and mix well. Chill in the refrigerator until serving time.

Pour the cranberry mixture into a punch bowl. Add scoops of the sherbet. Add the ginger ale and stir gently to blend. Ladle into punch cups.

ORIGINALLY PUBLISHED IN *Thymes Remembered*

THYME SAVER
For icy cold drinks that never get diluted, serve iced coffee, tea, or juice with ice cubes made from the beverage. Add herbs or edible flowers to the frozen cubes for even more flair.

Cranberry Pineapple Punch

SERVES 6

1 (48-ounce) bottle cranberry
 juice cocktail
1 (48-ounce) can pineapple juice
1/2 cup sugar
2 tablespoons almond extract
2 liters ginger ale, chilled

Combine the cranberry juice cocktail, pineapple juice, sugar and almond extract in a pitcher and stir until the sugar is dissolved. Pour into a large sealable plastic freezer bag. Freeze until firm. Thaw for 2 to 3 hours or until slushy. Place in a punch bowl and add the ginger ale. Ladle into punch cups. Small berries or fruit may be frozen in the cranberry juice mixture.

Chocolate Coffee

SERVES 12

3/4 cup sugar, or more to taste
2/3 cup instant coffee
1/2 cup chocolate syrup
2 quarts (8 cups) half-and-half
1/2 gallon coffee ice cream
1 (28-ounce) bottle club soda, or
 to taste, chilled

Mix the sugar, coffee, chocolate syrup and some of the half-and-half in a jar with a tight-fitting lid. Cover and shake well. Chill for 8 to 10 hours or days before serving, making sure the coffee granules are dissolved.

To serve, pour the remaining half-and-half and chocolate mixture in a punch bowl and stir well. Cut the ice cream into chunks and stir into the mixture. Add the club soda. As the ice cream melts, the full flavor emerges. Ladle into punch cups.

For additional flavor and presentation, serve in glasses and top with Homemade Whipped Cream on page 145 or top the punch with the Homemade Whipped Cream in the punch bowl. To keep cold, place ice in another larger punch bowl or big bowl and place underneath the coffee punch bowl.

ELIZABETH MOYA

Contributors & Testers

This cookbook is a collaboration of many people and could not have been created without the help of our supporters. Their hard work and thoughtfulness is greatly appreciated and makes this book a success. For those of you we have failed to thank by name, your contributions are no less appreciated and please accept our sincere apologies. We hope you enjoy this sampling of culinary delights.

Sincerely,

Betsy Caire Couch and

Gina Colley-Holgate,

A Thyme to Celebrate Chairs

Ellyn Aidman
Jen Anderson
Leigh Ansley
Betty Ashlock
Bettye "Bebe" Atkinson
Jackie Atwell
Randi Atwood
Kitty Ball
Kelly Barber
Eva Baxter
Sara Bayliss
Chef Grant Beane—Georgio's
Heather Beazley
Aggie Bell
Gail Bell
Paige Benton
Pat Beverly
Libby Bigham
Kristin Billingslea
Cathy Bishop
Margaret Black
Jennifer Blalock
Nancy Blum
Liz Bobeck
Ann and Elvis Boggan
Anne Wallis Bond
M. Michelle Bono
Peter and Kensy Boulware
Laura Pople Bracci
Peggy Brady
Stephanie Brandt
Flecia Braswell
Debbie Bergstrom Breeze
Kristen Bridges
Robyn Brock
Cassie Brooks
Marianne Brooks
Monica Browning
Martha Bryson
Tripp and Susie Busch-Transou
Alex Buss
John Buss
Chef Josh Butler
Darcy Byington
Dr. Michael Caire
Kitty Ball Camp
Cindy Campbell
Tina Campbell
Annie Carlson
Kathryn Cashin
Amanda Clements
Amy Cliburn
Brian Cliburn
Nancy Click
Kara Colley
Mike Colley
Sharon Colley

Cassie Willis Conn
Peter Cornais
Barbara Corven
Chris Couch
Cory Couch
Tina Couch
Carla Ferrell Cowles
David Cowles
Carole Cox
Jenni Cox
The Office of
    Florida Governor Charlie Crist
Anita Crockett
Sandy Crockett
Pep Culpepper
Connie Davis
John Dawson
Jenny Day
Marilyn Dean
Rebecca DeLaRosa
Beth Desloge
Heather Deyo
Rebekah Dorn
Juli Downs
Fran Doxsee
Elaine Drabik
Chef Tim Drown—University
    Center Club
Debbie Duffy
Clarissa Dunlap
Pam Edwards
Rick Edwards
Toni Egan
Judy Nicholas Etemadi
Lily Etemadi
Mireille Fall-Fry
Ginger Farrell
Sara Dean Faulkenberry
Chef Eric Favier—Chez Pierre
Desiree Fenniman
Anna Cam Fentriss
Frances Ferenchick
Janie Flack
Bill Flowers
Jeanne Clark Flowers
Heidi Floyd
Tricia Folsom
Linzy Foster
Dana Funaro
Denise Funaro
Natalie Ann Garner
Carla Ann Gaskin
Jessica Geib
Ezzie Goldman
Carol Atkins Goughnour
Shannon Grooters
Jane Grosslight

Chef David Gwynn—Cypress
Betty Gene Haller
Brooke Hallock
Heather Harrington
Boo Hartsell
Laurie D. Hartsfield
Wendy Hedrick
Megan Hensley
Sue Hightower
Calynne Hill
Rich Holbrook
Gregg Holgate
Margaret Holgate
Loranne Ausley and Bill Hollimon
Jill Hoover
Kendra Howard
R. Jai Howard
Kim Howes
The late Bea Huff
Suzanne Hughes
Whitney Hults-Richartz
Elizabeth Irvin
Kate Johnston
April W. Johnston
Karen Joiner
Melissa K. Joiner
Gerald Ensley and Sally Karioth
Molly Kellogg
Laura Ketcham
Allison Kinney
Mary Lee Kiracofe
Amy Simpson Kirby
Chef Brian Knepper—The
    Governor's Club
Tiffany Koenigkramer
Katerina Koikos
Anne Koios
Katie Kole
Michelle Lamar-Acuff
Alexis Antonacci Lambert
Kristin M. Large
Betty Lewis
Alex Loftus
Julie Lovelace
Jim Magill
Kelly Magill
Sara Marchessault
Mayor John and Mrs. Jane Marks
Ivette Marques
Sarah Zieman Martinez
Lori B. Mattice
Sarah Maxwell
Susan McAlister
Stephanie McCann
Beverly McCord
Jean McCully
Melinda McDaniel

Laureen McElroy
Rian Meadows
Marsha Medders
Cheryl Bosenberg Miles
Carrie Millar
Nancy Miller
Aleta Mitchell-Tapping
Gloria Morgan
Liz Morgenstern
Elizabeth Moya
Serena Moyle
Gjergj Ndoja
Hester Cowles Ndoja
Leah O'Connor
Elizabeth Oscar
Kathryn Oven
Terra Palmer
Annalisa Patrick
John Patrick
Lauren Shoaf Patrick
Nick Patronis
Sara and Jim Patterson
Audra Peoples
Andrea Personett
Vera Petersen
Melanie Phister
Amanda Porter
Joanna Price
Velma M. Proctor
Edith Purpura
Clifton Quinly
Melissa Reboso-Lombard
Brenda Rhinehart
Linda Richards—The Cake Shop
Clint Riley
Jean Rivers
Julie Kay Roberts
Sandy Roberts
Laura Rogers
Jenny Rosen
Lori Rowe
Katy Higgins Rudie
Allison Ruff
Saucy Catering
Lee Satterfield
Nella Schomburger
Wendy Sellers
Nora Sfarra
Sara Beth Shippen
Missy Shuman
Fran Simmons
Chef Art Smith
Dee Ann Smith
Gretchen Smith
Karen Smith
Kathleen Smith
Leslie Smith

Stephanie Smith
Amy Snook
Mary Jayne Sokolow
Stacey Speer
Leah Spencer
Brooke Spicer
Phyllis Stephens
Joyce Stillwell
Halley Stinchfield
Leah Stoetzel
Carole Strange
The late Evelyn Sykes
Kim Tabah
Janice Jordan Tesch
Susan Spratt Thomas
Amanda Karioth Thompson
Holly Thompson
Kent and Janet Thompson
Sam Thompson
Susan Thompson
Joanie Trotman
University Center Club
Susan Van Leuven
Erica Villanueva
Rise Villanueva
Kate Wasson
Dr. T. K. and Virginia Wetherell
Marie Webb
Tammy Webb
Caroline Weiss
Amanda Witters Whitaker
Mahaska Whitley
Martha Gene Wigginton
Representative Alan Williams
Ann Williams
Sarah Williams
Stephanie Williams
Tricia Willis
Carol Winger
Cindy Wise
Jennifer Womble
Laura Youmans
Eleanor Zieman
Dr. Stephen F. X. Zieman

Index

To order additional copies of

A Thyme to Celebrate

FRESH, CLASSIC RECIPES FOR ALL OF LIFE'S CELEBRATIONS

please contact us at
The Junior League of Tallahassee
850-224-9161
www.jltallahassee.org

Notes

Notes